Naive & Country Quilts

A Craftworld Book

Craftworld Books Pty Ltd
50 Silverwater Rd
Silverwater NSW 2128
Australia

First published by Craftworld Books Pty Ltd 1998

Managing Editor: Sue Aiken
Editor: Margaret Kelly
Designer: Vivien Valk Design

National Library of Australia Cataloguing-in-Publication data

Naive & Country Quilts.

Includes index.
ISBN 1 876490 00 4

1. Quilting.

646.21

Printed by Paramount Printing Co, Hong Kong

THE AUSTRALIAN
Country
CRAFT
SERIES
PRESENTS

Naive & Country Quilts

Craftworld Books

Contents

Hearts & Home

Farmyard Animals & Country Days

The Country Garden

Traditional Country Quilts

Acknowledgments

DEBORAH KITCHING
Naive Country Wall-hanging

A textile designer by trade, Deborah Kitching has combined this knowledge with a love of colour and fabric. In her naive work, Deborah breaks up the backgrounds into different colours to maintain a random look. Her skills are evident not only in the way she balances her colours and fabrics, but in the little surprises she includes.

DEB NICHOL
Golden Fleece

Deb Nichol is known for her country themes and colours. Her work ranges from highly saleable country quilts to bright, colourful pieces that owe their inspiration to the African–American style which advocates improvising, not measuring. The speed of this style of quilting so appealed to Deb that nearly all her work is now machine-sewn.

MARGARET MAHONEY
Hearts and Stars Quilt

For years Margaret Mahoney's work has encompassed traditional English hexagons and complex ancient Celtic knot designs, the subdued designs of North American Amish and the embellishing technique of appliqué. All are a showcase for her delicate and exact hand quilting. With her love of patchwork and quilting, Margaret's work provides the satisfaction of both challenge and creative pleasure.

BRIGITTE GIBLIN
Home is Where the Heart Is
Naive Pine Trees
Rustic Pinwheel Quilt

Brigitte Giblin began her quilting career with an appliqué sampler which she completed entirely by hand. Brigitte soon fell in love with the naive look of old quilts and now prefers to make quilts that look as if they were made fifty to a hundred years ago. These days Brigitte concentrates more on designing and teaching.

TITA LEACH
Country Woman's World
Farmyard Appliqué Quilt

Tita Leach was born and educated in Germany where sewing, embroidery and knitting were compulsory at school. Tita now alternates between making soft toys and quilting, often finding ways to combine the two.

Tita prefers hand appliqué, embroidery and quilting because of the close feeling that hand work gives her and because she finds it very therapeutic.

PAT WEIR-SMITH
Appletree Grove

Pat Weir-Smith began quilting at her local recreation centre. After making a number of full-sized quilts, Pat began specialising in machine pieced miniature quilts. She uses quick piecing techniques which involve no hand cutting or the use of templates. Pat now teaches patchwork and one of her most challenging classes is Baltimore quilt making.

JULIE WOODS
* Arkansas Troubles

Quilt artist, Julie Woods can't recall the number of quilts she has made and given away, but she still has an impressive collection. Julie, who has won many awards, enjoys the challenge of competitions, but more important to her is the enjoyment and learning that she gains from her patchwork quilting.

MARGARET SAMPSON
Naive Cushion

Margaret Sampson, quiltmaker and teacher, is respected for her generosity of spirit and thorough knowledge of technique and creativity. Margaret draws inspiration for her work from many sources, which is evident in the naive antique charm of her quilts. While she loves pieced work, Margaret particularly enjoys the freedom of appliqué work.

TRUDY BRODIE
* Shenandoah Floral Appliqué

A beautiful star quilt which she saw in the United States inspired Trudy Brodie to learn the creative craft of quilting.

Trudy has now emerged as a creative quilting talent and teacher. She believes that the techniques of piecing and quilting are important, but that colour and design are the true basis of an interesting quilt project.

HILARY SMITH
Primitive Country Farm

A lifelong passion for textiles and design has led Hilary Smith to the art of quilt making. Although much of Hilary's early work was in traditional designs and soft colours, she does not restrict her quilting to one particular style. Hilary now also enjoys designing naive and country-style quilts using country fabrics and flannels.

CHRISTINE BOOK
Hearts for Me
Hearth and Home
Sunbonnet Sue

A peep into the world of Christine Book offers an intriguing glimpse of colour and light. A self-confessed fabricaholic, Christine loves rich country colours, but in particular, the 1930s fabrics with their clear pastel shades and cheerful quirky patterns. Although Chris produces her share of large quilts, she particularly loves small projects because they are achievable for everyone.

KERRIE TAYLOR
Naive Dove Cushion

The inspiration for Kerrie Taylor's imaginative quilts comes from her peaceful surroundings. Palm trees shelter the house, a tropical garden attracts ducks and geese and a private rainforest is home to lorikeets and fantail pigeons.

Kerrie's quilts combine traditional cardboard template hand piecing techniques with inspirational designs, colours and fabrics in appliqué and embroidery.

CAROLINE PRICE
Classical Cats
Highways and Byways

Quilting and the country life are a perfect patchwork for quiltmaker Caroline Price. Combining her own creative work with finishing quilts for others, Caroline works mainly in pieced patchwork. She is now developing a more contemporary style with appliqué and exploring different areas of patchwork and quilting.

JILL GRIFFIN
Baa Baa Plaid Sheep

Jill Griffin's inspiration for patchwork started with pulpit hangings. She has always loved magazines and books and is fascinated by colours and the way fabrics work together, but she only began what she calls serious quilting a few years ago. Jill now designs projects and teaches beginners machine piecing as well as more-advanced techniques.

CHRIS HIGGINS
Floating Four-patch

A hexagon quilt which she made in the early seventies was the beginning of Chris Higgins' love affair with patchwork. Chris particularly loves machine piecing, especially the 1890s style of quilt design. She began teaching patchwork from home and now demonstrates and teaches her techniques at the Quilting Bee, at Gordon in Sydney.

PAULINE LOUGHHEAD
My Favourite Flannel Quilt

Pauline Loughhead has a particular love for quick piecing techniques and for country-style quilts. Since undergoing reconstructive hand surgery, Pauline is again able to hand quilt, to her delight. Pauline teaches patchwork and often travels to country areas where teaching is less accessible.

DOROTHY CLARK
Cottage Gardens Wall-hanging

Like all patchworkers, Dorothy Clark's great love is for fabric and colours. Dorothy enjoys all types of quilting especially naive and country. Her clever use of fabrics combined with appliqué is evident in the beautiful wall-hanging featured. It is also a great way to use those mountains of scrap fabrics we all collect.

LORRAINE MORAN
Rainy's Quilt
**Virginia Reel*

Lorraine Moran has been very active in the quilting world since the very early days of quilting in Australia. There was only one quilting shop in Sydney when she began. Lorraine has a wonderful eye for colours and loves to hand quilt. Lorraine's style can be described as traditional, but in a fun way.

FRAN WILLIAMS
Country Hearts

Fran Williams has a passion for fabric. After years of dressmaking, Fran discovered patchwork. She opened The Quilt Patch, at Launceston in Tasmania thirteen years ago and also teaches patchwork and hand appliqué. Fran's projects nearly always become teaching tools for her students.

* These projects are antique quilts. The Quiltmakers have written the instructions for their making.

Introduction

Naive and country style quilts give us a feeling of a lifestyle that is relaxed and comfortable, a simplicity reminiscent of bygone days. These quilts are an intimate, personal art form – a statement of a needleworker's love of fabric and thread and of the desire to give practical expression to her creative abilities.

In *Naive & Country Quilts*, we have included a wonderful range of projects from some of Australia's leading quiltmakers. Most of these talented women teach patchwork classes as well as indulging in their passion. This book, therefore, is not only for the experienced quiltmaker, but also for those who have admired this age-old skill and, until now, thought that it was beyond them.

There are beautiful colour photographs, easy-to-follow instructions, clear patterns and illustrations used throughout the book which will appeal to everyone. The pattern sheet includes those larger patterns which do not fit easily into a page size.

You will find a list of the necessary basic equipment, as well as the basic techniques required to successfully complete a quilt. A glossary of quilting terms explains the meaning of the words and phrases used in quilting and a conversion chart will help you with that precious fabric that is only 90cm wide. There is also a short profile of each of the quilters whose work is featured.

The projects are grouped into four theme sections. The theme for the first chapter is Hearts & Home. The second chapter tells of naive Farmyard Animals & Country Days. Chapter three is a myriad of flowers in The Country Garden and chapter four is filled with those Traditional Country Quilts.

The word quilt comes from the Latin word *culcita* meaning a stuffed sack, but it came into the English language from the French word *cuilte*. History tells us that the quilting of fabric was initially worked to provide warmth and to give comfort to the stitcher and her family. Today's quilter, however, is inspired by more than these basic necessities. For many people, quilting is simply an enjoyable hobby, but for just as many, it is an all-absorbing passion – as important to some as breathing and sleeping.

SECTION 1:
HEARTS & HOME

Each of the seven projects in this section is devoted to the heart and home theme. Included are two wall-hangings, two bed quilts, a wall quilt and a small quilt. You'll find crazy patchwork, hand and machine quilting, hand and machine appliqué, embroidery, machine piecing, cross stitch, instructions for working with flannel and tips on staining fabric.

SECTION 2:
FARMYARD ANIMALS
& COUNTRY DAYS

There is a quilt for every animal lover in this section – from the Primitive Country Farm scene to the sophisticated Classical Cats. We tell you how to recycle woollen clothing and how to felt the wool. You'll find strip-cutting construction techniques and also instructions for piecing blocks.

SECTION 3:
THE COUNTRY
GARDEN

Flowers are in abundance in this country garden. You can make a traditional Sunbonnet Sue wall quilt, appliquéd in reproduction fabrics; a Naive Cushion with instructions for appliqué techniques and prairie points; an elegant quilt featuring machine quilting on Naive Pine Trees; a lovely wall-hanging made from scrap fabrics with instructions for Broderie Perse; a mini-quilt made from tiny prints in antiqued colours which features the freezer paper method; and a charming floral appliqué quilt with a swag border.

SECTION 4:
TRADITIONAL COUNTRY
QUILTS

For the country quilt lover, this section features seven magnificent bed quilts. Instructions for traditional blocks such as Remembrance, Arkansas Troubles, Jacob's Ladder, Virginia Reel, Floating Four-patch and a pinwheel block are given here, as well as hints on flannel, trapezium borders and an 8-pointed star.

All in all, *Naive & Country Quilts* offers you practical information and inspirational projects to warm your heart and your home.

METRIC/IMPERIAL
MEASUREMENTS

Important

Fabric requirements are provided in both metric and imperial measures.

All fabric requirements are based on a minimum width of 115cm (45in).

The instructions for each project are provided in the measurements used by the quilter.

ENLARGING
THE PATTERNS

Most patterns in this book need to be enlarged before use. To do this accurately, look for the photocopy symbol and number on the pattern (for example ⊟130%), set the photocopier to the percentage given and photocopy each piece on this setting. Patterns that have the symbol ⊟ SS do not need enlarging.

The History of Quilting

The term 'patchwork' conjures up images of those colourful scrap quilts made by pioneer women to help their families survive icy northern winters. Indeed, it's a craft that has survived the ravages of time. Not only are many of the best examples of pioneer quilts hanging in galleries and museums around the world, but modern women (and some men) are continuing to make fine examples of patchwork art.

The history of patchwork, in fact, goes back much further than many imagine. Examples of patchwork have been uncovered in Egyptian tombs dating back to 980 BC, and there is evidence that during the Middle Ages, quilted clothing was used for military wear. In Europe and the United Kingdom, patchwork was not widespread until the seventeenth and eighteenth centuries and this coincided with the availability of printed cotton fabrics from India.

Most of us, however, identify most strongly with the patchwork made by the early American settlers. In fact, many of the traditional patterns taught and made now were designed by these pioneer women and some have their origins in specific historic occasions and celebrations. Thrift and necessity are behind many of the antique quilts still admired today. Poor availability of fabrics meant that anything and everything was used – from feed sacks to old garments – in the making of warm bedcovers. When the cotton industry took off in the southern states, patchwork really came into its own and a tremendous range of fabrics was suddenly available to inspire more imaginative and creative work.

In Australia, the history of patchwork is not as rich, due to the much warmer climate and the lack of cotton fabrics. Wool is traditionally the primary industry and it wasn't until imported cotton came onto the market in the last century that patchwork became popular.

Now, of course, it's a pastime enjoyed by thousands all over the country.

There is something very special about opening the door of a house and being welcomed by a treasured quilt. It may be one made by the owner, or a bush pioneer from days of old. It may have been found in the trash and treasure stall at the local church fête, or handed down from a beloved relative. Whatever the case, it's our connection with the past that draws us to these tangible treasures.

What we call country quilts are the quilts of yesteryear; the ones that women toiled over with time and care; the ones we attempt to re-create today using traditional blocks and reproduction fabrics.

The dictionary definition of 'naive' means having or showing natural simplicity of nature. There is much greater freedom with naive appliqué than you would find with traditional Baltimore quilts, for instance.

Many pieced blocks lend themselves to a country theme – Churn Dash, Ohio Star, Baskets, Log Cabin, Flying Geese, Drunkard's Path, Broken Dishes and Dresden Plate. The Schoolhouse block in particular is a favourite motif, symbolising the spirit of the country. Then there are the strippy quilts, designed to use up whatever fabric is available, challenging the quiltmaker to design within the limitations of her scrap stash.

People, farm animals, country houses, vases of flowers and hearts and hands copied from children's simple drawings are ideal for naive quilting. Some quilt makers take the process one step further by appliquéing naive shapes over their pieced blocks.

Today's quilters have the benefits of iron-on fusible webbing to make the look of naive quilts quick and easy to achieve. With edges left raw, quilters are free to finish the images with bold embroidery stitches, emphasising the outline and adding to the naivete.

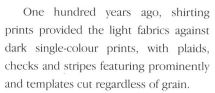

COUNTRY DECORATING

While quilts were originally designed for warmth and colour in a bedroom, even in the early days quiltmakers found creative uses for their handiwork throughout the home. A decorative quilt would cover a table in the centre of the room and quilts were used as curtains, covers for chests and radiators, draught stoppers and protective coverings for armchairs.

Many a worn or unappealing item of furniture has found new life with a quilt covering. Cushions made from quilt blocks are both utilitarian and objects of beauty. Even a single block can be framed or finished with binding and hung on the wall with a decorative hanger.

Quilts are a powerful decorating tool. Depending on the style of quilt, they can establish the whole tone and colour scheme of a room through the impact of their bold designs and dramatic colours. They can also act as a more subtle, versatile accent.

The choice of quilt patterns is also important when you want to make a particular style of quilt. Country fabrics are busy and strong in colour so do not confuse the issue by choosing a complex pattern or intricate appliqué.

One hundred years ago, shirting prints provided the light fabrics against dark single-colour prints, with plaids, checks and stripes featuring prominently and templates cut regardless of grain.

The tiniest scraps would be pieced together to make bigger pieces, or another fabric, similar in colour but not the same would be used. Pieced blocks were separated with plain blocks or sashing and borders were simple strips. Elaborate quilting patterns were left to masterpieces. Simple designs worked best in this style.

With naive appliqué, there is greater freedom than with traditional appliqué. Naive style quilts are more open and airy than pieced country quilts.

Appliqué shapes for country quilts should be simple and not too small. Remember that these quilts are generally utility quilts so farm animals, barns and houses, sunflowers and bird houses are particularly appropriate.

Quilts in the naive style are more open and airy than pieced country quilts. The naive look we all admire in old quilts came as a result of women attempting a fine quilt only to find they did not have the resources or means to complete their projects to perfection and so had to compromise by using scraps.

When featuring the country look, differentiate between storage and display. Bring your quilts out at different times of the year and move them around.

Naive and country quilts typify a way of life that appears relaxed and comfortable, a simplicity reminiscent of bygone days. They are an intimate, personal art form – a statement of a needleworker's love of fabric and thread and the desire to give practical expression to their creative abilities.

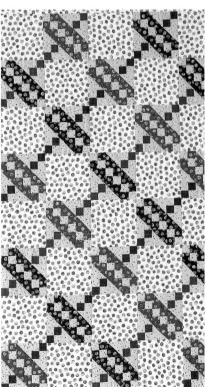

Techniques

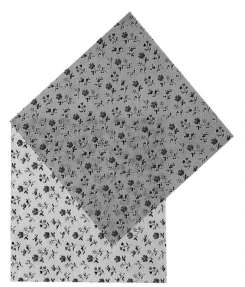

COUNTRY COLOUR

❖

Country quilts are immediately identified by colour and you can choose whatever colours appeal to you. In fact it is an unexpected colour combination that adds simplicity to a country theme.

Colour selection should be inspired by nature's hues. It is the warm browns and yellows of a sunburnt country, the greens of tree and paddock, the blues of sky and ocean and the glowing hues of sunset reds and wildflowers that are the harmonising colours of country.

Choosing fabrics for country quilts is made easy today with entire ranges devoted to the country theme.

TO AGE FABRICS

❖

Tea-dyeing tends to dull fabrics and give them a mellow sepia tone. As with most forms of dyeing, tea-dyeing works best on 100 per cent cotton fabrics that have been pre-washed to remove any manufacturer's sizing, finishing or polishing agents.

Listed below are several different methods of tea-dyeing.

1 Place half a dozen tea bags in hot water for fifteen minutes. Remove the tea bags and add the fabric. Leave it to soak for thirty minutes, then rinse it in cool water and hang out to dry.

Sprinkling tea directly onto the wet fabric gives an uneven, speckled effect.

2 Place four tablespoons of instant coffee and eight tea bags in two litres of hot water. Let the tea bags soak for several minutes, then remove them and immerse the fabric. Allow it to soak for thirty minutes, or longer for stronger dye. If you prefer a patchy look, leave the tea bags in the solution. Rinse the fabric and dry.

3 Parisian essence, used for gravy browning, can be used as a fabric stain in place of tea or coffee in either of the above methods. Iron the fabric to set the dye.

4 Using a plastic bucket, pour in a litre of hot water. Add three heaped teaspoons of instant coffee, three or four tea bags and two or three tablespoons of vinegar. Add enough cool water to bring the mixture to hand-hot and immerse the fabric. If you want an even stain, ensure the fabric is immersed and swirl it around in the bucket for a few minutes. Leave to soak for a few hours for a darker shade. Remove fabric and rinse it in cold running water. Dry in a clothes dryer and press with a steam iron.

5 To achieve a speckled look, sprinkle tea leaves directly onto the wet fabric using about one teaspoon per 25cm (10in) of fabric. Roll up the fabric and place it in a plastic bag. Microwave on high for about one minute or leave the plastic bag in the sun for a few hours. Shake off tea leaves and rinse.

6 A novel technique is to wash the fabric in the dishwasher. The abrasiveness and bleach that is in the dishwasher detergent dulls the colours and 'wears' the fabric.

Once your fabric is dry, it may need more variation. If it does, pour the tea-dye mixture into a spray bottle and spray on a few extra splotches.

Use your clothes dryer to permanently crush, or grunge the fabric.

CRUSHING FABRIC

This process is also called grunging. Unlike tea-dyeing, fabric with a lot of sizing or stiffening in it works best for this process. Wet the fabric and squeeze it into a tight ball, squeezing out as much water as you can. Place the ball in the dryer on the hottest setting possible. Once the ball is dry right through to the centre, remove it and allow it to cool.

If the fabric is not stiff enough to hold together in a ball until it is dry, try tying it around a few times with string.

NOTE: Do not use rubber bands in the clothes dryer.

Iron the fabric flat for accurate cutting. After this grunging process, the crinkles in the fabric should not come out when the fabric is ironed.

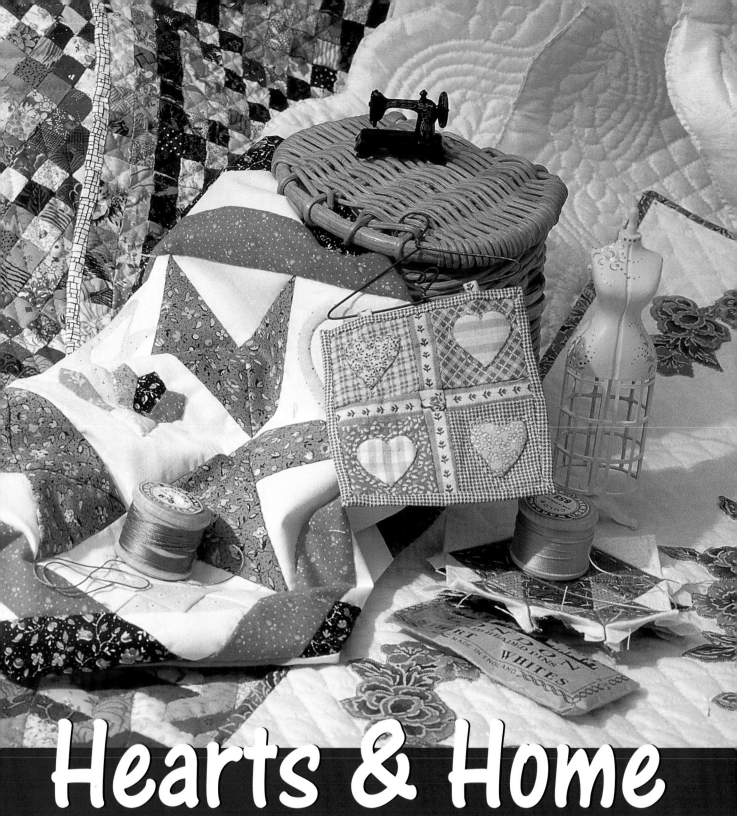

Hearts & Home

For thousands of years, the heart has been one of the most powerful and frequently used symbols. Today, the heart is still a popular motif for appliqué and patchwork quilts. In early colonial days, women used their ingenuity to provide warmth and decorative touches to their homes. The home became the symbol of hope and the inspiration for their quiltmaking.

Home Is Where the Heart Is

*This delightful country style wall-hanging combines crazy patchwork,
appliqué and embroidery techniques. The use of scraps,
checks and tiny floral fabrics enhances the naive look, while
Suffolk Puff flowers add a final touch.*

PREPARATION

CENTRAL BLOCKS

From the background fabric cut four 8½in squares. Using the patterns provided, cut out the templates for the house pieces and heart shape. Remember to add ¼in seam allowance when cutting out appliqué pieces. You will need to make two house and two heart blocks.

CONSTRUCTION

APPLIQUÉ

For each house, appliqué the windows onto B. Appliqué the door to C. Sew together A and B by hand or machine. Sew C to AB. Appliqué the house to a background square. All the appliqué is worked using a blind stitch with a thread that matches the top fabric.

CRAZY PATCHWORK HEARTS

Begin with a 2in square. Cut off one corner. Sew narrow strips of fabric approximately 2in wide around this centre square. It is made in the same way as a log cabin but with five sides. Follow the sequence shown in Diagram 1 and continue in this manner until the block is large enough to cut out the heart shape using the template provided.

HELPFUL HINT

When cutting the strips to use around the centre piece, the sides of the strips do not need to be parallel but the sides MUST be straight or the heart shape will not lie flat.

FINISHED SIZE

- 56cm (22in) square

MATERIALS

- 30cm (⅓yd) background fabric for the blocks
- 40cm (½yd) fabric for the borders
- 30-40cm (⅓-½yd) assorted light and dark scraps for appliqué and piecing
- 70cm (¾yd) backing fabric
- 70cm (¾yd) batting
- 20cm (¼yd) fabric for binding
- Template plastic
- Embroidery thread
- 2B pencil
- Neutral sewing thread
- Quilting thread
- Buttons (optional)
- Scissors and pins

NOTE: For appliqué patterns, add a seam allowance of 6mm (¼in) when cutting out shapes. Appliqué should be completed using a blind stitch with thread to match the top fabric. Turn under the seam allowance as you sew each piece onto the background fabric.

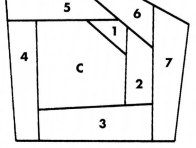

Use small prints and florals for the house appliqué and add an embroidered heart above the door.   **Diagram 1**

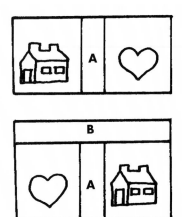

Diagram 2

Continue adding strips around the central five-sided piece until the block is large enough to cut out the heart shape.

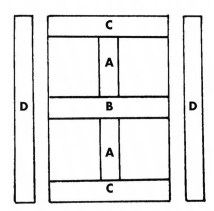

Diagram 3

BORDERS

❖

For the A borders, cut two pieces 2½in x 8½in and B border 2½in x 18½in. Attach these borders as shown in Diagram 2. Cut two C borders 3½in x 18½in and two D borders 3½in x 24½in. Attach all these borders as shown in Diagram 3 opposite.

SUFFOLK PUFF FLOWERS

❖

Make six Suffolk Puff flowers approximately 1in in diameter by cutting 2in circles of fabric. Turn the raw edge of the fabric over and stitch a running stitch around the edge of each circle and pull it into the centre. Iron the puffs flat and stay stitch into place along the centre A borders as shown. Embroider the stems and leaves in back stitch using three strands of embroidery cotton (see Diagram 4). Alternatively, use old-fashioned buttons for the flower heads.

Diagram 4

EMBROIDERY

❖

Mark lightly with a pencil, then embroider across the centre B border the words, HOME IS WHERE THE ♡ IS using three strands of embroidery thread in your colour choice. Embroider a heart shape onto each house above the doors as shown on the template patterns on page 23.

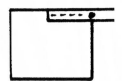

Stop ½in from the corner, back stitch and take out of the machine.

Fold binding up on a 45 degree angle and fold on corner.

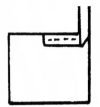

Fold binding down level with the edge. Sew along edge to next corner and repeat.

Diagram 5

QUILTING

❖

Baste or pin the three layers of quilt top, batting and backing fabric together. Quilt around the houses and hearts, then around each block ¼in in from the seams.

Mitre all the corners as shown in Diagram 5. Repeat for all four corners.

Overlap ends and cut off excess binding. Fold binding to the back and slip stitch along the back using a thread to match binding. Press your work. Add a rod pocket to the back of quilt and your wall-hanging is ready to hang up and enjoy.

FINISHING

❖

**ASSEMBLY
AND BINDING**

Trim the edges of the quilt. Cut and join three, 3in wide strips to make a 99in length for binding. Press this in half and sew onto the front of the quilt with all raw edges together, ½in in from the edge starting at the centre bottom.

Add seam allowance

SS

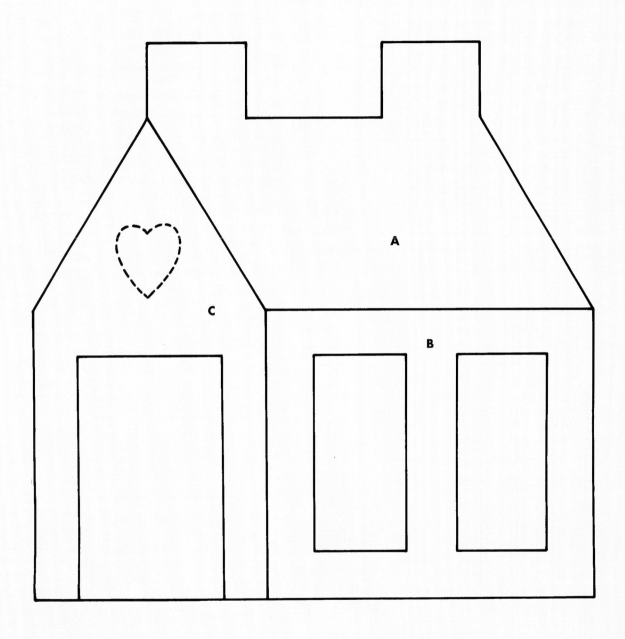

A

C

B

Hearts and Stars Quilt

This quilt is made from cream homespun and a variety of checks to produce a country look. It is made up of eighteen Star and seventeen Heart Blocks and combines machine piecing, simple hand appliqué and hand quilting. Almost every star and heart is made from a different check or stripe.

PREPARATION

HEART BLOCKS

Cut out the background blocks a little larger than the finished size of 30cm square, because the appliqué can slightly reduce the size of the block. It is a simple process to cut the finished block back to size.

Mark the location of the hearts on the background block using a sharp pencil. Use three hearts to get the placement you like. Remember that you are going to sew this block to a star block, so don't place the hearts too close to the seam line.

CONSTRUCTION

APPLIQUE

The following appliqué instructions use the English paper method, but use any other technique if you prefer, such as freezer paper, needle turning, hand or machine appliqué.

For each heart you will need a 15cm square of fabric, and there are fifty-one hearts required in all.

Cut out the paper shapes using the full sized template provided (old greeting

FINISHED SIZE

- 170cm x 210cm (67in x 83in)
- Block size 30cm (12in)

MATERIALS

- 4.2m (4³/₄yd) homespun for the top
- 3.8m (4¹/₄yd) for backing
- 3m (3¹/₃yd) various checks and stripes
- Batting to suit
- Thread to match fabrics
- Quilting thread
- Fine sharp needle for appliqué
- Size 10 betweens needle for quilting
- Rotary cutter and board
- Patchwork ruler
- HB pencil
- Cardboard
- Plastic heart shape template
- Quilting hoop
- 6mm (¹/₄in) masking tape

NOTE: This project has been designed using metric measurements.

Step 1
Tack the fabric onto the templates, gently easing the fabric around the shape.

Step 2
Appliqué the heart shapes onto the background fabric using small stitches.

Diagram 1
Cutting the Star Block.

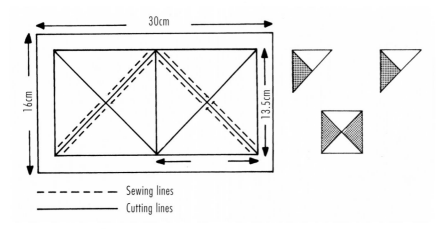

When you get close to the cleavage at the top of the heart, snip down to the paper. (Don't snip too soon, or the line of the cut may end up in the wrong place.)

When you are ready to appliqué the heart onto the background, use an iron to press the covered piece. Remove the tacking and cardboard and pin the heart to the background. To sew on the shape, start with a knot and bring the needle up from the bottom through the appliqué piece, close to the edge. Take the needle back down close to where it came up – not further ahead as in hemming. Use a thread to match the heart, not the background. The stitches should be placed quite closely together. Make seventeen Heart Blocks.

STAR BLOCKS

cards, cereal boxes and manilla folders are all useful).

Cut the fabric, leaving a 6mm seam allowance and baste the fabric onto the paper shapes. Use a paper clip to keep the fabric in place rather than pins, as these can cause bubbles in the fabric.

Begin tacking on the long side, using your thumb to ease the fabric slightly.

For the corner squares of the Star Blocks, cut seventy-two 11.5cm homespun squares. For the centre of the blocks, cut eighteen 11.5cm check or stripe squares.

The points of the stars are made by machine sewing the background and check or stripe fabrics together as follows.

On the homespun, mark out a 30cm x 16cm rectangle as shown in Diagram 1. Pin the marked homespun to the check or stripe fabric. Sew along the broken lines, which are 6mm from the diagonal. Use scissors to cut on all the solid lines.

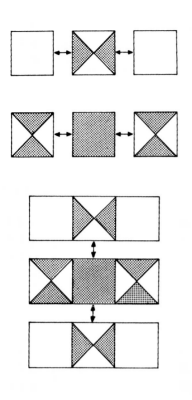

Diagram 2
Assembly of the Star Block

Step 3
Cut triangles for the points of the stars using two pieces of fabric sewn together.

Press all the seams towards the check or stripe fabric and join two sets to make a square. Each block has four sets of points.

Join the squares into rows, then join the three rows together to make a block as shown in Diagram 2 above. You will need to make eighteen Star Blocks in all.

ASSEMBLING

You should now have eighteen Star Blocks and seventeen Heart Blocks to make up the quilt top. Trim all the blocks carefully to make them the same size. Join them together into rows following the layout given in Diagram 3.

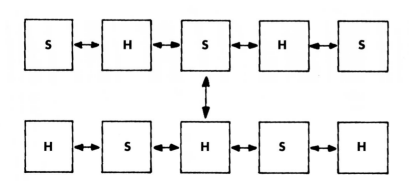

Diagram 3
Assembly of the quilt top

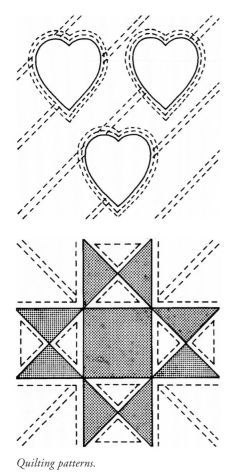

Quilting patterns.

Finally, join the rows to make the quilt top, minus the border.

BORDERS

Cut the remaining pieces of check and stripe fabric into 10cm strips. Cut these into a variety of lengths – squares, long and short rectangles. Join these together in a random order to make strips the length and width of the quilt. Measure through the centre of the quilt, rather than the actual borders, to get the lengths you require. Join the borders to the quilt top.

BACKING

Remove selvedges from the backing piece. Cut in half across the fabric width. Join the two pieces to make a 220cm x 180cm sheet. The seam will be horizontal.

QUILTING

Sandwich the top, batting and backing, then baste the three layers together. The quilt can now be hand or machine quilted. If hand quilting, use a hoop to keep the tension even. Quilting thread should match the homespun.

Betweens are short needles which help you make small stitches. The quilting stitch is a running stitch, worked from the front of the quilt. If sewing through many layers – for example, at a seam – you can use a stabbing technique. Push the needle through to the back of the quilt, then push it back to the front. The back of your quilt should look like the front, but this will require practice. The finer the needle the easier it is to make small stitches. If you haven't hand quilted before, try a No 9 needle, or if you are experienced, you might prefer to use a No 12 needle. Quilting lines are 6mm apart. Use 6mm masking tape to mark the lines. See the quilting suggestions shown on this page.

For quilting around the appliquéd pieces, quilt 6mm from the edge of the heart, then 3mm inside these lines, closer to the heart. You can either judge these lines by eye or pencil them in. Try to get your stitches even, but don't worry too much about their size or the number of stitches per centimetre.

FINISHING

BINDING

Trim the edges of the quilt. Cut a 6cm wide binding from the homespun fabric. Cut it on the straight. You will need to join strips together to form a strip long enough to go around the quilt. The joins are less obvious if you make them on the bias and are also less bulky when sewn onto the quilt.

Fold the strips in half lengthwise, wrong sides together. Match the raw edges of the quilt and the folded binding and sew to the front of the quilt. Mitre or butt the corners. Fold the binding to the back of the quilt and slip stitch in place.

Label and sign your quilt.

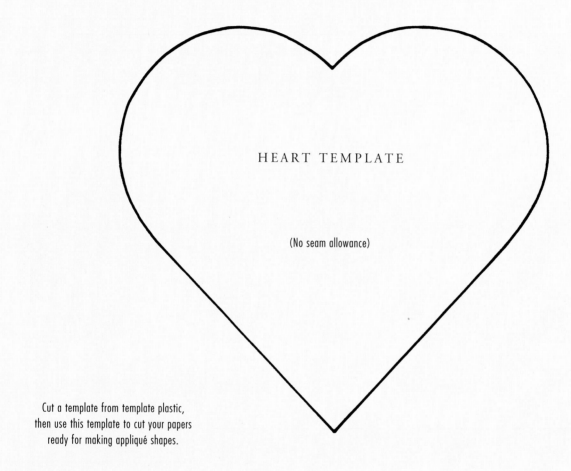

HEART TEMPLATE

(No seam allowance)

Cut a template from template plastic,
then use this template to cut your papers
ready for making appliqué shapes.

Hearts for Me

*Appliquéd naive hearts made from a variety
of scrap flannels add a charming touch
to this soft, warm flannel quilt. Recycle your favourite
flannel garments for a personal touch.*

FINISHED SIZE

- 128cm x 154cm (50in x 60½in)

MATERIALS

- 45cm (½yd) of 12 flannel prints
- 45cm (½yd) plain cream flannel – to be stained to a caramel shade
- 30cm (⅓yd) bright accent colour (red) for inner border
- 1m (1⅛yd) dark flannel (brown) for outer border
- 40cm (½yd) dark-coloured flannel for binding
- 3m (3⅓yd) flannel of choice for backing
- 140cm x 170cm (55in x 67in) quilt batting (wool batting was used to enhance the soft feel of the quilt)
- Grey or brown cotton thread for piecing
- Matching thread for quilting
- Matching thread for binding
- Thick embroidery thread (dark green and dark blue) for embroidery details on hearts
- Cardboard or template plastic (optional) OR 10 degree wedge rule
- Rotary cutter
- Mat and ruler
- Sewing machine and general sewing supplies

NOTE: Due to the scrap nature of this quilt, it is best to select a range of different prints including checks, stripes and florals. Be sure to include light and dark prints in your collection.

PREPARATION

Due to the slightly stretchy nature of flannel, it is advisable to pre-wash and soak all fabrics separately in warm water (detergent is not necessary). Leave them to soak for a while to check for any dye loss, especially from the darker fabrics. At this stage, you may need to replace some of the fabrics. Dry the fabrics in the clothes dryer, then press them carefully with a steam iron.

This process will help to firm up the fabric's weave and remove any excess dye. A 112cm (44in) wide fabric can lose up to 10cm (4in) in both length and width from washing.

STAINING

If staining the plain cream flannel to achieve a caramel shade, do it as a whole piece before cutting. Using a plastic bucket, pour in a litre of hot water and add three heaped teaspoons of instant coffee, three or four tea bags and two or three tablespoons of vinegar. Add enough cool water to bring the mixture to hand-hot and immerse the flannel. For an even stain on the fabric, take care to ensure the fabric is entirely immersed and swirl around in the bucket for a few minutes.

Leave to soak for a few hours if you want a darker shade. Remove the fabric from the stain mixture and rinse it in cold running water. If the fabric still seems too light, immerse it again in the stain mixture and leave it to soak for longer. Rinse well. Dry in the dryer and press with a steam iron. If you prefer an uneven antique effect for the stain, use less water with the stain mixture and scrunch up the fabric when immersing.

CUTTING

A ¼in seam allowance is used throughout this project and is included in the cutting measurements.

This quilt can be cut out in one of two ways – using the templates provided or using a 10 degree wedge rule.

TEMPLATE METHOD

Trace the template onto template plastic or cardboard and cut out carefully. Remember that the template includes a ¼in seam allowance. Position the template on the back of the fabric, following the grainline and trace around it using a sharp lead pencil or a permanent fabric marker. Cut along this line with scissors or a rotary cutter. To make the best use of the fabric, position the template in a 'top and tail' fashion along the grainline.

WEDGE RULE METHOD

Using a rotary cutter and a 10 degree wedge rule will speed up the cutting process. Cut one or two 5½in wide strips across the width of the twelve print fabrics. Use the 10 degree wedge rule to cut the trapezoid shapes (approximately ten shapes per strip). Place the 5½in wide strips on the cutting board and line them up at the 19¼ and 13¾ marks on the wedge rule with the cut edges of the strip. Use the rotary cutter to slice on either side of the wedge rule, to produce the trapezoid shape. To make the next cut along the strip, without wasting any fabric, turn the rule around and align it on the edge you have just cut (see step-by-step photograph).

Whichever method you choose, cut one hundred and twenty of the trapezoid shapes in an assortment of light and dark

flannels. Cut twenty half-size trapezoid shapes, or cut ten more trapezoids, then cut through their length to yield twenty half-shapes. These may be cut from strip left-overs or cut separately.

These half-trapezoids are used at either end of the pieced rows that form the body of the quilt's design.

RED INNER
BORDER

Cut five 2in strips across the width of the fabric. Cut one strip in half and attach it to one full strip. Repeat with the other half-strip. You should now have two longer border strips and two the width of the fabric.

BROWN OUTER
BORDER

From the dark border flannel cut five strips, 6½in by width. Cut and piece the strips to equal two strips 6in wide by 41½in long from the dark flannel; make two strips 6in wide by 51½in long.

Step 1
Cutting the trapezoids from the 5½in flannel strip using the 10 degree wedge rule. Place rule on fabric between the 19¼ mark and the 13¾ mark. Cut, then turn rule around and cut the next trapezoid.

TIPS ON WORKING WITH FLANNEL

Cotton flannel fabric is not difficult to work with if it is pre-washed prior to cutting. Follow the instructions below for successful sewing.

- Ensure you are working with a sharp needle. Always use a new needle after six to eight hours of sewing.

- Use only 100 per cent cotton thread. Polyester thread may distort on ironing and may pucker the seams.

- Clean your machine as you go and apply oil if necessary. Flannel tends to shed fluff as you sew which can clog the bobbin.

- Press seams only after the top of the quilt is finished. Do not press the flannel as you go as this can cause some of the pieces to stretch.

- When pressing flannel, use a hot steam iron and press down firmly. Don't move the iron back and forth.

- Flannel makes a great design sheet as fabrics cling to it. Lay out the pieces for the quilt top on a flannel sheet and arrange them to ensure you have a satisfying distribution of colours.

- Choose blocks with a simple construction such as a Square in a Square which can be measured and trimmed each step of the way. This will cut down on the amount of stretching.

- Don't limit yourself to patchwork flannel fabrics. Flannelette shirts, pyjamas, children's flannelette and hand-dyed flannels can all be put to good use. Try recycling favourite old shirts to give a personal touch.

- Grainline is very important. Make sure the outside edges of the quilt are cut on the straight, not the bias.

- Forget about matching plaids. It's too difficult because of the loose weave, and mismatched plaids have a charm all their own.

- Stitch a practice block first to get used to working with the flannel.

NOTE: The border strips have been cut wider than the finished size of 4¼in, because the flannel fabric is inclined to fray. To allow for this, it is best to attach a wider piece of fabric than is necessary and trim it back to size, after the quilting is completed.

CORNER SQUARES

For the caramel-coloured corner squares in the outer border, cut four 6in squares from the flannel that has been stained with the mixture of tea, coffee and vinegar. As these squares form part of the border, they will be cut down to the finished size after they have been quilted.

Set aside the remainder of this fabric for the appliquéd hearts.

BINDING

Cut six 2½in wide strips across the width of the dark coloured flannel.

CONSTRUCTION

❖

PIECING

This quilt design uses a one-patch pattern that depends on a balanced arrangement of lights and darks. Before sewing all rows together, lay out the pieces on the floor or pin them to a design wall (a flannelette sheet is good for this) and re-arrange them to achieve a pleasing overall look, with an even distribution of lights and darks.

The main body of the quilt is made up of ten rows of the trapezoid-shape. These rows are constructed by alternating the placement of the trapezoids (see step-by-step photograph).

After laying out the shapes and re-arranging them to ensure a balance of lights and darks, sew the trapezoids into rows made up of twelve full shapes with a half-trapezoid at either end.

Step 2
Trapezoids arranged ready to sew in rows, with a half-trapezoid at the end.

Pin the trapezoids together carefully to ensure they do not stretch on sewing.

Make ten rows the same. Sew the rows together in pairs, then the pairs together. Finally, join the two halves of the quilt. For successful construction, ensure that the rows are pinned well, points match and the seams lock in place.

ASSEMBLY

RED INNER BORDER

Using the cut strips, pin the top and bottom borders to the quilt. Establish the centre point and pin towards each corner. Sew, then repeat for each side. Press carefully so that the seam allowance faces away from the centre of the quilt.

OUTER BORDER
*(wide dark border with
light corner squares)*

Because flannel tends to stretch, measure the quilt through the centre both ways first and adjust the border measurements if necessary. Pin from the centre point to the corners, then stitch the top and bottom dark border strips in place. To each end of the longer side strips, attach the cream corner squares. Again, pin from the centre first and match the corner squares exactly with the top and bottom borders. Stitch these long side borders in place. Press the seam allowance back towards the centre of the quilt.

APPLIQUED HEARTS

Now that the flannel quilt top is pieced together, you can randomly appliqué any number of caramel naive hearts into position. Hearts can be appliquéd either way – by template or flipped.

Using the heart pattern, cut a light cardboard template and cut out the number of hearts you require from the caramel-stained fabric, adding ¼in seam

Step 3
The naive heart appliquéd onto a trapezoid block. Thick embroidery thread is used for the primitive stitching.

allowance all around to turn under. Baste the fabric to the template using large running stitches.

Position the heart and pin it to the selected block. Use small appliqué stitches around part of the heart. Remove the cardboard shape and complete the stitching. Each heart may be further embellished by embroidery. Some hearts are outlined in simple running stitch, while others are detailed in a contrasting naive stitch, using a thick embroidery thread.

BACKING

When cutting the backing fabric for the quilt, it is more economical for the lengths of fabric to run across the quilt. Cut the lining fabric in half crosswise. Cut one of these lengths (selvedge to selvedge) in half lengthwise. Attach these to either side of the full length.

QUILTING

Layer the quilt top, batting and backing fabric. Wool batting has been used in this quilt, but cotton batting can be used instead as the flannel will also cling to it well. Baste as you prefer. Hand or machine quilt the layers together. This quilt has been machine quilted in the ditch around the trapezoids, in the ditch around the borders and with three rows of quilting in the borders, each 1¼in apart. Alternatively, the quilt can be tied with thick thread at each intersection to match the embroidery. Keep the tied ends to the back of the quilt. A combination of machine quilting and tying would also be effective. This quilt doesn't need to be too heavily quilted.

Once the quilting is completed, trim the quilt so that each border is approximately 4¾in or 5in wide.

FINISHING

BINDING

Sew the binding strips together, end to end. Fold the binding in half lengthwise, wrong sides together. Line up the raw edges of the binding and the quilt, right sides together and sew to the right side of the quilt using ⅜in seam allowance. Mitre the corners and fold the binding to the back. Hand appliqué in a thread that matches the binding. Label your quilt on the back.

On pages 14 and 15 you will find several different techniques for fabric dyeing. Follow the instructions carefully to ensure a good result.

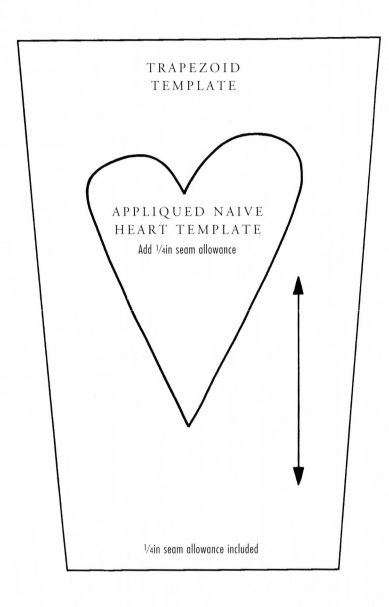

TRAPEZOID
TEMPLATE

APPLIQUED NAIVE
HEART TEMPLATE
Add ¼in seam allowance

¼in seam allowance included

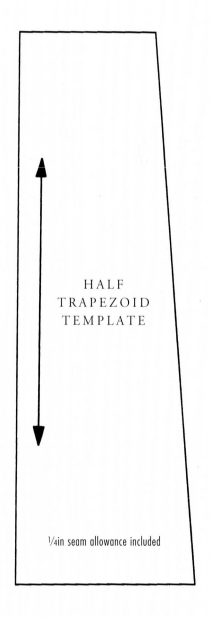

HALF
TRAPEZOID
TEMPLATE

¼in seam allowance included

SS

Country Woman's World

*This naive country sampler with its
country-style flannels and appliquéd pieces
imaginatively captures the activities
of country life.*

PREPARATION

CUTTING

From the thirteen flannel quarters for the blocks, choose twelve for the surrounding blocks and one for the background for the central House Block. Set aside the fabric for the central block as this will be cut later.

Cut an exact 12in square of cardboard and position this template on a flannel quarter. Trace around the template on the reverse side of the flannel, with a marking pen or pencil. Ensure that the sides follow the grainline of the fabric. This will be your stitching line. Mark a ¾in seam allowance outside the stitching line to allow for any fraying while the appliqué motifs are being stitched in place. Cut out the block along this outside line. Cut out twelve blocks in this manner. Set aside any flannel remaining after cutting these blocks for the sixteen appliqué hearts.

THE MOTIFS

After deciding your colour placement for the blocks, select the colours for the country motifs. Start with the simpler motifs first and build up colour combinations. For the Three Trees Block, choose three contrasting greens and three contrasting orange/browns. Keep experimenting with colour combinations until they look 'right'. Use a photocopier to enlarge the patterns on the Pattern Sheet and trace them onto Vliesofix.

NOTE: Remember to add extra to pieces when pattern pieces overlap. Study the photograph of the quilt and note where pieces will need to be cut longer than the pattern. For example, trunks extend under the foliage, honey and jam jars under the jam covers, petals under flower centre, spools and handle under the sewing machine.

Always trace onto the smooth side of Vliesofix. Leave at least ¼in margin around the pencilled shape when cutting out ready for bonding to fabric. Label the Vliesofix shapes as you trace them to avoid mixing them up.

Place a Vliesofix shape onto the back of the selected fabric, checking that no edges overhang the fabric. When satisfied with the position, press onto the fabric, using an appliqué mat to prevent damaging the iron's surface. Once the two surfaces have bonded, cut carefully around the pencil shape. Repeat for any other shapes needed to complete the motif. Peel off the backing paper and arrange onto the flannel block.

Repeat the Vliesofix method of appliqué for all twelve blocks.

When all the motifs are bonded to the blocks, appliqué around the motifs using ecru crochet cotton and a tiny Buttonhole Stitch (not a Blanket Stitch) as this will give a more secure edge to the motif. Completely stitch around each motif.

When the blocks are completed, add any additional stitching such as the lines on the parsnip, the face and limb outlines on the cow, sewing machine name and embellishments, the writing on honey and jam pots. Set the blocks aside.

Central House Block

The finished size of this block will be 13in square. From the fat quarter set aside, cut a 14½in square, keeping the grainline parallel with the edges. From the cotton print, cut a rectangle 8½in x 5½in for the house. Trace the windows, the door, the frames, the chimneys and the house onto Vliesofix, remembering to add extra to those pieces which will be laying underneath others. Iron them onto the fabrics you have chosen and cut them out. Complete the lower part of the house by arranging the windows, frames and door on the house section, then peel the paper backing off these pieces and iron them onto the fabric in the required position.

FINISHED SIZE

- approximately 126cm (50in) square
- Block size 30cm (12in)

MATERIALS

- 14 fat quarters of flannel fabrics as background for blocks (13 for blocks, one for the first border around the central block/motif)
- 12 fat quarters of cotton print, plus additional scraps for motifs
- 90cm (1yd) cotton ticking for the second border and binding – (border 30cm (12in), binding 60cm (24in)
- 2.7m (3yd) non-directional cotton print or 2m (2¼yd) directional cotton print for backing
- 153cm (60in) square of batting
- 1.5m (1¾yd) Vliesofix (rolled, not folded)
- Thin A3 size cardboard, for traditional appliqué (hearts, verandah)
- No 60 crochet cotton for appliqué Buttonhole Stitch
- Dark brown cotton for outlining hearts and top stitching motifs
- Sewing cottons to match fabrics, for traditional appliqué (hearts, verandah)
- 8 black doll buttons for the eyes of cats, cow, sheep
- 12 x 2.5cm (1in) wooden buttons for button-tied block intersections
- 4 x 1.5cm (⅝in) wooden buttons for border block intersections
- Embellishments such as buttons, ties, etc, to add your own personal touch of country
- Sheet of thick cardboard to cut a 30cm (12in) square template for the twelve outer blocks
- Marking pen, chalk or lead pencil
- Appliqué mat
- Template plastic

NOTE: All fabrics must be pre-washed, dried and pressed before use.

Roof

This section uses a foundation piecing technique. Photocopy the foundation layout roof pattern piece. Using a combination of four colours, cut ten strips 1½in x 5in. Select the first two strips and place right sides together on the blank side of the paper pattern. Hold the paper up to the light to ensure the pieces cover the first section. Pin to hold in position. Place with paper side up on the sewing machine and stitch directly onto paper along the line between the two first sections, using a very small stitch length. Fold open the two strips of fabric and place the third strip in position, again holding it up to the light to check that it is in the correct place. Sew along the line. Continue adding strips of fabric until the roof is completely covered. Machine around the outline of the roof to hold it in place and to indicate the turn-under line. Separate the fabric from the paper.

Trim the roof to ¼in from the stitch-outline line. Turn this under and baste it in place to hold it in position. Place on the block and pin. Place the chimneys in position with raw edges under the roof and the walls of the house extension under the roof. Centre all pieces. Peel off the backing paper and iron on Vliesofix appliqué shapes. Place and tack the roof in position. Invisibly appliqué stitch into place. Buttonhole Stitch around the chimneys, doors, windows, frames and outlines of the house.

Verandah

The verandah section uses traditional appliqué to attach the pieces. First, cut the templates from template plastic, then use the template plastic to cut two large and two small verandah posts out of thin cardboard. Place the templates face down onto the back of the fabric and pin them in place.

Cut out the fabric, leaving ¼in seam allowance around the edge of the card. Turn over the hem and baste it in place. Repeat for all four posts. Iron in the crease. Remove the basting and cardboard. Set aside.

Fence rail and posts

Choose two contrasting fabrics. Cut enough 1¼in wide strips to provide four rails and six posts. Fold under both edges, making a strip ½in wide. Arrange the posts, rails and end posts, so that the rails and posts tuck underneath each other. Pin firmly in place and using matching cotton, appliqué stitch all the rails and posts in place. The centre panel is now complete.

FIRST BORDER

From the fat quarter of flannel set aside for the first border, cut four strips 1½in wide. Trim back the centre panel to 13½in square. Using a ¼in seam, add the side borders first, then press the seam out and trim. Add the top and bottom border and press again.

SECOND BORDER

Cut two strips 5in x the width of the fabric. You will need 15½in long strips for the top and bottom borders. Attach to the first border using a ¼in seam. Press. Cut both the side borders 24½in long, sew and press.

HEARTS

Make a template from template plastic and cut sixteen hearts out of thin cardboard. Place these templates face down onto the back of the selected scraps of flannel fabric, and pin them in place. Cut out the fabric, leaving a ¼in seam allowance around the edge of the cardboard. Turn over the hem and baste in place. Press in the crease. Remove the basting and cardboard. Centre the hearts on the second border as shown in the construction diagram. Pin in place and using an invisible appliqué stitch, sew the hearts in place.

NOTE: Nick the 'V' of the heart as you reach it, not before.

CONSTRUCTION

ASSEMBLY

Lay out the twelve panels on the floor in order. Refer to the construction diagram and stitch the four top panels together (section A). Join the two side panels (two B sections). Attach the four lower panels (section C). Join the central panel (section D) to the two sides.

Align the top four-panel row to the central block, matching seams. Repeat for the lower panel row. Press the seams out.

BACKING AND BATTING

Make up the backing and batting to extend 2in out from the completed quilt top. The number of joins needed will depend on which fabric and batting you use. Layer the backing, batting and quilt panel together. Tack with a large zigzag to hold it in place.

BINDING

Do not trim the batting at this stage. Cut five strips 5in wide across the width of the cotton ticking set aside for the binding. Cut one of these strips into four equal lengths and add each one to the end of each of the four remaining long strips. Press the seam open. Fold each length in half lengthwise, with the wrong sides together and press.

Attach the binding to the front of the quilt, stitching the sides first. Machine in place using a ¼in seam, making sure the sewing line is along the edge of the pieced quilt and 1in from the edge of the batting and backing. Trim the batting to 1in from the sewing line. Fold the binding to the back and slip stitch in place.

Repeat for the top and bottom bindings, leaving extra fabric at the end of each binding strip to turn under to neaten the corners.

QUILTING

Using a running stitch and dark brown quilting cotton, stitch around each heart and motif to hold the layers together.

FINISHING

Place buttons on the panel joins. See the photograph for placement. Place black doll buttons on the animals' faces. Include any other embellishments if you wish to add your own personal touch.

Quilt construction
Position the hearts on the second border as shown. Stitch the top four panels together (section A). Join the two side panels (two B sections). Join the four lower panels (section C). Attach the centre panel (section D) to the two sides, then add top and bottom sections.

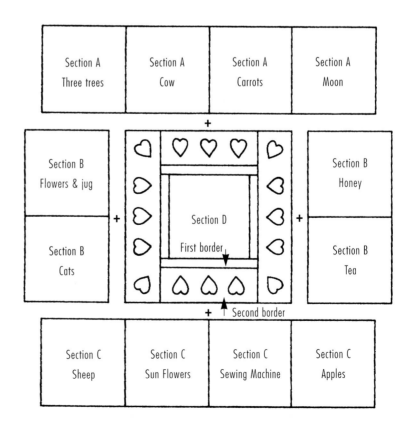

Naive Country Wall-hanging

*This little naive wall-hanging in check and stripe country colours
is quick and easy to make and would make a special gift
for family or friends. Embroider the year at the top of your project
as shown, or leave it plain if you prefer.*

PREPARATION

CUTTING

For the background, cut four 6½in squares from four different light to medium fabrics.

For the side borders, cut two 2in x 12½in strips from the dark check fabric, and for the top and bottom borders, cut two 2in x 15½in strips, also from the dark check fabric.

CONSTRUCTION

ASSEMBLY

It is important to use an exact ¼in seam allowance throughout, to line up the raw edges carefully and to pin where necessary when you are machine sewing. Using a warm to hot iron, press the seams toward the outside borders.

Sew the four background squares together into a square, then add the side borders, followed by the top and bottom borders. The block should now measure 15½in square.

APPLIQUE

Using the pattern provided, trace the appliqué shapes in reverse onto the paper side of the Vliesofix, allowing for a ⅛in overlap where necessary. Leave at least ½in space between each tracing.

Cut out each shape about ¼in out from the traced line. Iron the shapes onto the wrong sides of your chosen fabrics, then cut them out carefully on the traced line.

Peel the backing paper away and following the pattern, arrange the pieces carefully onto the background square, underlapping where necessary.

FINISHED SIZE

• 38cm (15½in square)

MATERIALS

• Assorted fabric scraps for backgrounds and appliqué
• Assorted Coton Perlé No 5 thread
• Vliesofix
• 46cm (18in) square of coordinating backing fabric
• 46cm (18in) square of Pellon or thin batting
• Black quilting thread
• Quilt hanger

The designs on each square will vary slightly.

When you are happy with the arrangement (always double check), fuse the design to the background with a medium iron.

EMBROIDERY

Using a No 5 Coton Perlé thread, Blanket Stitch around all the raw edges in colours which complement your chosen fabrics.

Feather Stitch over the border seams. Trace the year onto the background and work it in Stem Stitch. If you don't want to put the date on your quilt, you can work a name or quotation in Stem Stitch where the date would appear.

Stitch a small star in Straight Stitch onto the centre of each bud and a large star in each corner.

Don't be concerned if your stitching is not perfect or the stars are not all the same size, as this will add to the naive character of the wall-hanging.

QUILTING

Sandwich the backing fabric, Pellon and appliquéd top together and pin or baste the three layers together.

Using the black quilting thread, outline the quilt around all the appliqué shapes to create an interesting background. Quilt a random zigzag stitch along each of the border strips. For those who want added interest, the house design and the corner pieces can also be quilted in the manner you desire.

FINISHING

Once the quilting is completed, carefully trim back the batting until it is the same size as the appliquéd top. Be careful not to trim the backing fabric at this time.

Using a rotary cutter and ruler, trim the backing fabric carefully so that it is a $\frac{1}{2}$in wider on all sides than on the appliquéd top of the quilt. Bring the excess backing fabric to the front of the block and turn under a scant $\frac{1}{4}$in hem to form the binding.

Stitch the hem in place using No 5 Coton Perlé and a small running stitch.

Make a label for the back and sign and date your wall-hanging.

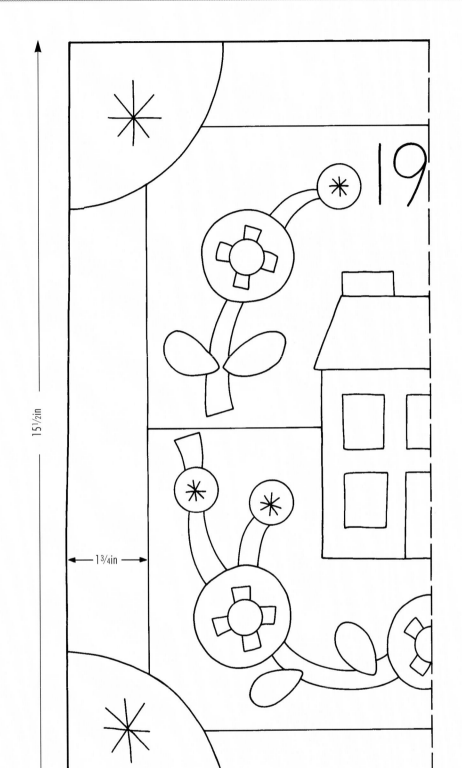

15¹/₂in

1³/₄in

19

1996

Mirror reverse to complete pattern.

 200%

Hearth and Home

The folk art style of the eighteenth century cross stitch samplers
was the inspiration for this charming appliquéd wall quilt.
This naive project depicts objects from everyday life —
hearts, birds, flowers, leaves, trees, and also the home.

PREPARATION

Osnaburg

From the osnaburg, cut one piece 4½in x 15in for section A; one piece 6½in x 15in for section D.

First cream/beige print

From the first cream/beige print, cut one piece 3in x 15in for section B.

Second cream/beige print

From the second cream/beige print, cut one piece 5in x 15in for section C.

Third cream/beige print

From the third cream/beige print, cut one piece 8½in x 15in for section E.

Light ticking stripe fabric

For the first border, cut two 6in x 15in strips from the light ticking stripe fabric to make the top and bottom of the centre panel and cut two 6in x 36½in strips or cut them the length of the quilt.

NOTE: The ticking stripe runs vertically through all border pieces, so ensure that the pieces are cut taking account of this direction.

Brown fabric for the outer border and bindings

For the outer border and bindings, cut eight 2in strips across the width of the fabric from the brown fabric.

From one of the fat quarters of green fabric, cut four 1in wide bias strips.

From the second fat quarter of green fabric, cut two 1in wide bias strips.

CONSTRUCTION

PIECING THE BACKGROUND

Using ¼in seam allowance, stitch sections A through E together and add

the first border before applying the appliqué. Refer to the diagram below. Attach the top and bottom borders first, then the sides.

NOTE: This border is slightly larger than the finished size. The extra fabric used allows for handling while the appliqué is being stitched.

Try to keep the appliquéd designs at least ½in from the edge of the borders all the way around.

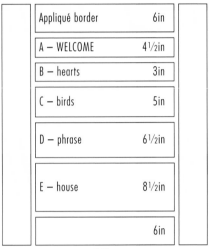

Diagram 1
Hearth and Home quilt construction

APPLIQUE

The traditional or English method of appliqué has been used in this design, though you may prefer to stitch using the method of appliqué with which you are more familiar. Trace all the appliqué pieces from the Pattern Sheet onto template plastic and cut them out.

Place the shapes to be appliquéd onto the lightweight cardboard, then trace around and cut out the required number of fabric pieces according to your own choice of colours and prints.

Centre Sampler

For the centre sampler, you will need five hearts, three birds, two trees and one house shape.

FINISHED SIZE

• 71cm x 98cm (28in x 38½in)

MATERIALS

• 4 light-coloured fabrics for background

• 20cm (¼yd) Osnaburg (sections A and D)

• 10cm (⅛yd) cream/beige print (section B)

• 15cm (¼yd) second cream/beige fabric (section C)

• 25cm (⅓yd) third cream/beige fabric (section E)

• 1m (1⅛yd) light-coloured ticking-type stripe for first border

• 50cm (⅔yd) brown fabric for outer border and binding

• Scraps of assorted prints and colours for appliqué

• 2 fat quarters of two different green fabrics for the appliquéd stems

• 85cm (1yd) fabric for backing

• 85cm x 105cm (33½in x 41½in) thin batting

• Cotton thread for piecing background and threads to match fabrics for appliqué

• Cream quilting thread

• Embroidery threads Coton Perlé No 5 for WELCOME, Coton Perlé No 8 for wording, brown thread for decorative Cross Stitch

• Small appliqué needle

• Template plastic

• Lightweight cardboard for appliqué templates

• Embroidery hoop and embroidery needles No 7 or 8

• Sewing machine, scissors, pins, pencil

NOTE: All fabrics should be 100 per cent cotton, 112cm (44in) wide, pre-washed and ironed. A 6mm (¼in) seam allowance is used throughout and is included in the cutting measurements.

STITCHES USED

Appliqué Stitch, Back Stitch, Running Stitch,

Decorative Cross Stitch

1 *Cardboard appliqué templates.*
2 *Pieces tacked to cardboard templates
   ready to appliqué.*
3 *A completed flower.*
4 *Bias seams for appliqué.*

Border Design

For the border design, you will need two vases, ten flower shapes, fourteen petals and two centres for the seven-petalled flowers, six leaves, the large heart and the hand and heart.

Place each cardboard shape face down on the back of the appropriate fabric and pin it in place. Cut out the shapes, allowing ¼in seam allowance.

Using needle and thread, fold the seam allowance firmly over the edge of the cardboard and baste through the fabric and the cardboard. As you baste the seam allowance in place you will need to gather it slightly to ease the fullness. If necessary, clip the curves as you go. Check the right side of the fabric shape to ensure that the work is smooth and firm. Press the shape (see step-by-step photograph).

Appliqué the shape into position, using a matching thread, a small appliqué needle and hidden slip stitch. Where possible, remove the cardboard template prior to completing the appliqué. If you think you will lose the shape of the fabric piece being appliquéd, complete the appliqué stitching, then remove the basting from the shape and make a small diagonal slit in the back of your work from which you should be able to carefully remove the cardboard template.

To make the bias strip for the vine design, join two of the strips together to form one long bias strip. Carefully fold the strip into thirds along its length, pin, then baste into place, taking care not to stretch the strip.

Once you have made two long lengths of bias strips in this manner, pin, then appliqué them into position using the photograph of the quilt given as a suggested arrangement. Add in shorter flower stems made from the second green fabric as you go.

EMBROIDERY

Using the featured designs, trace the words to be embroidered into the correct position, using a sharp lead pencil or fine point permanent fabric marker. For best results, use an embroidery hoop and embroidery needle size 7 or 8.

Complete all words to be embroidered in an even back stitch, using the thicker thread for the word 'WELCOME'. The No 8 thread is used for all the other words. A thinner thread is used to work

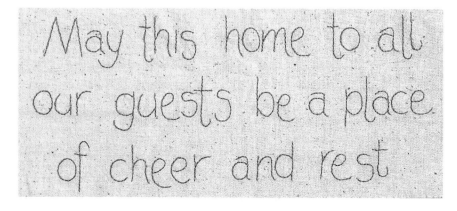

the decorative cross stitches all around the centre panel.

BORDERS

Carefully press the quilt top, lay it on a flat surface and using a rotary cutter, ruler and board, square up all edges. Cut back the border to a width of 5½in. Ensure the top and bottom measurements are the same and that both side measurements are equal.

Measure the length and width through the centre of the quilt top. Cut the brown border strips to these measurements. Pin these strips to top and bottom, right sides together, then machine-stitch in place.

BACKING

The quilt backing is made from a slightly larger length of fabric, about 3in, right around the quilt. This fabric is approximately 35in x 44in.

QUILTING

Sandwich the backing, batting and quilt top together and then pin or baste the three layers using your preferred method. The pictured quilt has been hand quilted in the ditch between the blocks of the centre panel, using a thread to match and also between the first and last border of the quilt. You may wish to incorporate quilting stitches around the appliqué motifs as well. Trim any excess backing and batting so that it is level with the top.

FINISHING

BINDING

Fold, then press the four binding strips in half, with wrong sides together. Stitch to the front of the quilt using a scant ¼in seam allowance and mitred corners. Fold the binding to the back and slip stitch into place.

Make a label for the back of the quilt and sign and date it.

Country Hearts

With a combination of hand appliqué and machine piecing, this hearts design can be adapted to quilts big or small and the block can be incorporated into a sampler quilt. Rotary cutting and strip piecing makes the sashing easy to construct and tied quilting enhances the country look.

PREPARATION

Pre-wash and iron all fabrics. All the templates and measurements include ¼in seam allowances. Please read all the instructions carefully before commencing. All pieces are sewn using a ¼in seam allowance. Block size is 9½in including seam allowance.

TEMPLATES

Remember that all the templates have a seam allowance included. Refer to the pattern provided and make templates for A, B, C and D.

CUTTING

Hearts

From each of the six prints, cut one complete heart. You will need two each of A, C, and D, one of B and one of B reversed (eight pieces).

HELPFUL HINT

Fold the fabric double to cut all pieces and you will get B and B reversed. They can all be cut by guiding the rotary cutter carefully around the templates.

Trace B template guide onto freezer paper, making six each of B and B reversed. (Fold the paper in half to cut two each time.)

Sashing

When cutting the strips for the sashing, ensure they are all cut across the fabric selvedge to selvedge.

From the A plain fabric (½yd), cut five strips, 2½in wide.

From the B plain fabric (⅝yd), cut ten strips, 1½in wide and one strip, 2½in wide.

From the print fabric for the sashing, (¼yd), cut two strips, each of which is 1½in wide.

CONSTRUCTION

NOTE: Use ¼in seams throughout.

HEARTS

Lay out each block to give good contrast between the pieces. Each block requires eight pieces and you will have six contrasting fabrics that will need to be placed so that no two are connecting.

Iron the freezer paper B guides to the wrong side of each of the B fabric pieces. Line up the edges of the corners and you will have ¼in seam allowance around the curve only.

Tack the seam allowance down over the edge of the freezer paper, easing to fit the curve. Aligning the corners, hand appliqué a B piece on the top of an A, using a thread that matches the B pieces. Stitch only on the curved edge, leaving the straight sides open. Pull out the basting stitches and remove the freezer paper. Repeat with the other side of the heart. Sew the tops of the heart together and press the seams to the right.

Sew all Cs to Ds in a gently curved seam. Press the seam towards D.

Sew the heart bases together. Press the seams to the left (see photograph).

Sew the top units to the bottom units. You will have six hearts; each should measure 9½in. Trim all the squares to the same size if needed. Remember, if it differs from 9½in, you will need to cut the sashing to match this measurement.

Press the centre seam towards the bottom of the quilt.

Sashing and Nine-patch Corner Squares

There are two different units which form the sashing of the quilt.

Unit 1

Sew a 1½in B plain strip to either side of a 2½in A plain strip.

FINISHED SIZE

- 97cm x 130cm (38in x 51in)
- Block size 24cm (9½in)

MATERIALS

- 20cm (¼yd) of six contrasting prints for the hearts
- 40cm (½yd) plain A sashing
- 60cm (⅔yd) plain B sashing
- 20cm (¼yd) print for sashing
- 90cm (1yd) print for borders and binding
- 110 cm x 140cm (42in x 56in) fabric for backing
- 110cm x 140cm (42in x 56in) medium loft batting
- Three skeins of embroidery thread to tie quilt
- Thread to match fabric for appliqué and piecing
- General sewing supplies
- Rotary cutter and mat
- Quilter's ruler

NOTE: All fabric measurements are based on 115cm (45in) wide fabrics.

Construction of the Heart Block sections.

Press the seams towards the outside edges. Cross-cut into seventeen pieces 9½in long (or the length of your block size) for the sashing.

Cross-cut the remaining pieces of these sets into twelve lengths, each 2½in for the nine-patch corner.

Unit 2

Sew a 1½in C plain strip to either side of the 2½in B plain strip.

Press the seams towards the centre and cross-cut this set into twenty-four pieces, each 1½in. Sew a 1½in Unit 2 piece to either side of a 2½in Unit 1 piece. Press the seams towards the outside edge. You will now have twelve nine-patch corner blocks.

ASSEMBLY

Referring to the quilt layout in the photograph, arrange the hearts, sashing and nine-patch corner blocks. Sew these into rows, then sew the rows together to form the centre of the quilt

BORDERS

Cut four 4½in fabric strips from the border piece.

Measure through the centre of the quilt from top to bottom to ascertain the measurement for the side borders. Join two sets of two strips together and cut two borders to this length.

The pieces left over will be used for the top and bottom borders.

Attach the strips to the sides, pinning carefully and press the seams towards the outside edge.

Measure side to side through the centre for the top and bottom borders, cut, attach to the sides and press towards the outside edge.

QUILTING

Press the top of the quilt firmly. Layer the backing, batting and quilt top and firmly baste or pin them together. Quilting can be done by machine, hand or tied.

The featured quilt has been tied with six strands of embroidery thread, using a colour that matches one of the fabrics in the sashing.

TYING THE QUILT

Thread the needle with a long length of thread; do not knot the end. Take small stitches through all layers from the top, using the intersections of the seams as a guide for placement. Pull up the thread, leaving 3in of tail. Do not cut the thread. Move to the next tie position and take another small stitch through all layers, leaving a long, loose length between the tie positions on the quilt top.

Cut each length of thread between stitches, leaving 3in of thread for tying. Any less and it will be awkward to tie a knot. Use a reef knot, left over right, right over left, then trim the tails to 1in. Vacuum the top of the quilt or take it outside and shake it to remove any thread scraps.

FINISHING

BINDING

Cut five strips of fabric each 2½in. Join the binding strips into one length, and press in half with wrong sides together. With all raw edges together, stitch the binding to the front of the quilt, folding the corners in mitres. Turn the binding to the back of the quilt and firmly slip stitch it in place.

Don't forget to label and date the back of your quilt.

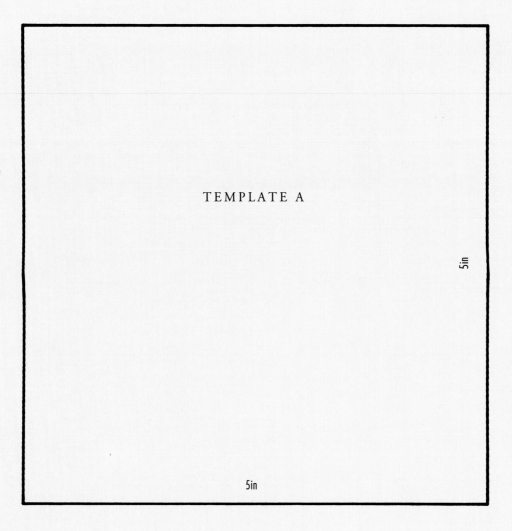

TEMPLATE A

5in

5in

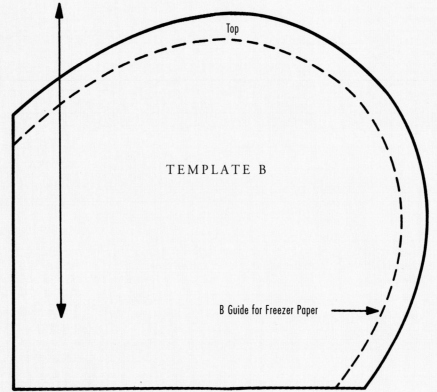

Top

TEMPLATE B

B Guide for Freezer Paper

SS

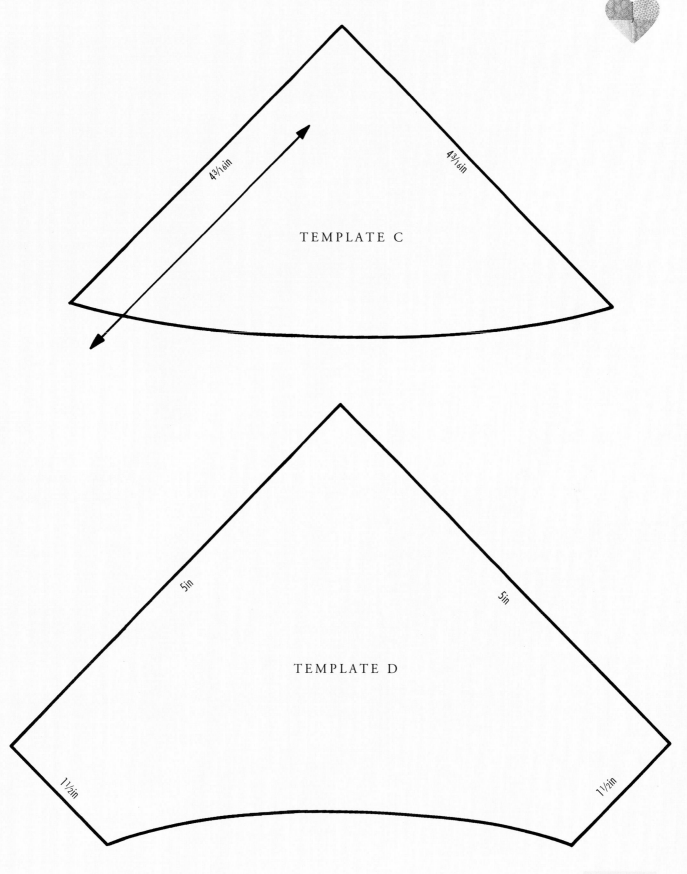

TEMPLATE C

4³/₁₆in

4³/₁₆in

TEMPLATE D

5in

5in

1½in

1½in

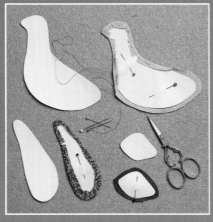

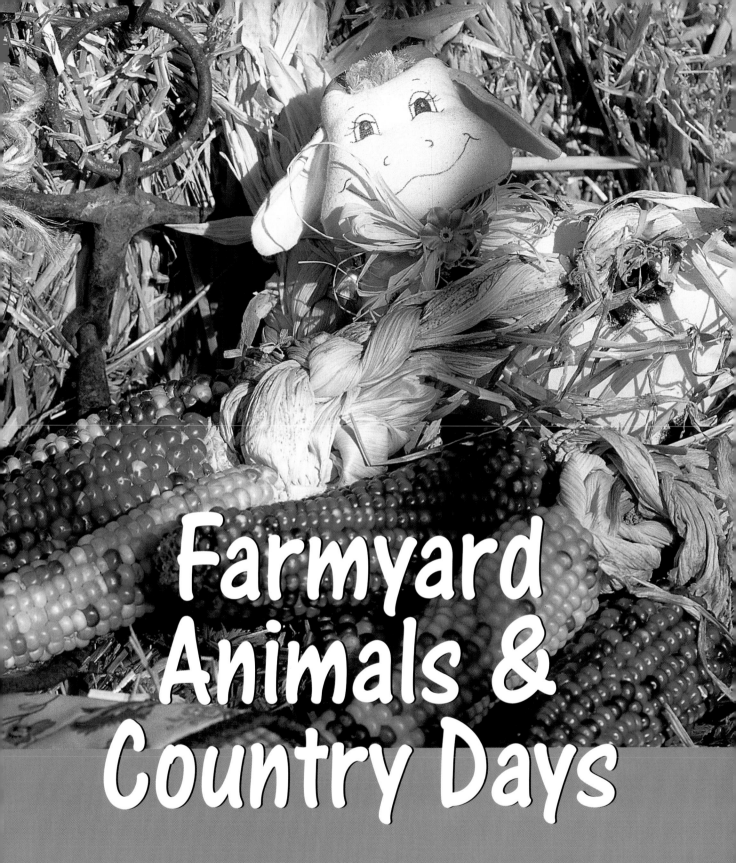

Farmyard Animals & Country Days

Farmyard animals have come to represent tranquillity, stability and friendship and have been a source of artistic inspiration for hundreds of years. They have proved a popular link to the land which was the basis of rural heritage. Light-hearted and faithful, these motifs carry a message of continuity between country and city, family and friends, past with present.

Primitive Country Farm

This delightful little wall-hanging sized quilt would take
pride of place on the wall in any home.
It cleverly combines appliqué and pieced blocks with
a variety of country style fabrics and motifs.

PREPARATION

CUTTING

Black fabric

From the black fabric, for block 13, cut one piece 10½in x 6½in; block 12, cut one piece 5½in x 5½in; block 2, one piece 3½in x 6½in, block 10, one piece 5½in x 1in. For the borders, cut two pieces 35½in x 4½in and two pieces 22½in x 4½in.

Check fabric

From the check fabric, for the inner borders, cut two pieces 1½in x 20½in and two pieces 1½in x 27½in. For the bindings, cut two pieces 1½in x 31in and two pieces 1½in x 35in.

Also from the check fabric, cut the following. Cut one piece of fabric 1½in x 4½in, six pieces 1½in x 5½in, three pieces 1½in x 6½in, one piece 1½in x 9½in and one piece 1¾in x 8½in.

Refer to the layout diagram on page 61 for the placement of these pieces. See pages 64 and 65 for pattern pieces except for the tree, house, barn and flying geese which appear on the Pattern Sheet.

From various scraps of your choice

From your choice of scraps, for block 1, cut one piece 6½in x 2½in; block 3, refer to the template shapes and cut four pieces of template A (two in reverse), cut two pieces of template B, two of template C and one of template D; block 4, cut one piece 7½in x 5½in; block 5, cut one piece 4in x 6½in; block 6, cut one piece 4in x 6½in; block 7, cut one piece 8½in x 7½in.

Referring to the template shapes, for block 8, cut two pieces of template 3 (one in reverse) and one each of the remaining templates; block 9, cut one piece 6½in x 5½in; block 10, cut one piece 4½in x 5½in and cut one piece 1in x 5½in.

For block 11, refer to the template

shapes and cut five of template A and ten of template B (five in reverse); block 14, cut one piece 4½in x 5½in; block 15, and again referring to the template shapes, cut three pieces of template A in one fabric and in reverse in different fabric, cut also one piece each of template 1, 5, 6, 7 and 8 and two pieces of template 2, 3 and 4 (one in reverse).

NOTE: Template 6 and 8 are appliquéd on to template pieces 5 and 7 respectively before they are pieced; for block 16, cut one piece 2½in x 6½in.

Cut the remaining appliqué pieces from the patterns provided. With the pieced blocks, piece them together in rows, then join the rows.

HELPFUL HINT

With so many pieces being cut for this quilt, it is a good idea to put each of the pieces into separate plastic bags and label them accordingly.

CONSTRUCTION

APPLIQUE

Appliqué the sunflowers, stars, sheep; the large trees and trunks of the small trees; the cows, rooster, ducks, girl and the small flowers using Vliesofix and Buttonhole Stitch.

To use Vliesofix, trace the reverse of the shape required onto the paper side of the Vliesofix. Cut out the shape, leaving space outside the marked line.

Place the shape, adhesive side down onto the wrong side of the fabric and press to bond. Cut out the shape along the marked line.

Remove paper backing and position the shape onto right side of background fabric, adhesive side down, and press. Buttonhole Stitch around each shape with one strand of embroidery cotton.

FINISHED SIZE

• approximately 76cm x 89cm (30in x 35in)

MATERIALS

• 1m (1⅛yd) black fabric for blocks and borders

• 1m (1⅛yd) check fabric for borders

• 25cm (⅓yd) yellow fabric for sunflowers

• 25cm (⅓yd) green fabric for sunflower stems and leaves

• Assorted scraps of fabric for other background and appliqué pieces

• 1m (1⅛yd) Vliesofix (fusible webbing)

• 1m (1⅛yd) batting

• 1m (1⅛yd) backing fabric

• 3 skeins black stranded cotton

• 1 skein stranded cotton, the colour of your choice for tying quilt

• 5 assorted buttons

• 4 matching buttons for cows' eyes

NOTE: Instructions include 6mm (¼in) seam allowance.

Two forms of appliqué are used.

Block 3

Piece the two small triangles (B) to each side of the large triangles (A), then join the two large rectangles (C) to each side of the smaller rectangle (D).

Join in rows, then add the checked border beginning with side pieces (1½in x 5½in), followed by the 4½in piece to complete Block 3. Refer to the layout diagram.

Block 4

Vliesofix the stars in place and Buttonhole Stitch around the shapes.

Blocks 5 and 6

Vliesofix the sheep and the tree trunk to the background fabric, appliqué the hearts into place, then Buttonhole Stitch around the shapes.

Block 7

Join the check side pieces to the background fabric, then Vliesofix the cows and trees in position and Buttonhole Stitch around each shape.

Block 8

Join pieces 2, 1 and 4 in a row, join pieces 3, 5 and 3 (reversed) in a row, join pieces 6 and 7, then join these to 8.

Join the three rows and appliqué the heart shape (9) onto piece 8.

Block 9

Vliesofix the girl to the background and Buttonhole Stitch all the raw edges.

Fray two small pieces of fabric and using large stitches, sew these pieces onto the dress to make patches.

Add a few extra details of Straight Stitch at the underarm and from the neck of the apron to indicate creases.

Using six strands of embroidery thread, make knots for the girl's hair leaving the ends as long as you please.

Make small embroidery thread bows and stitch them to each side of her head.

For the hearts and small trees on blocks, 1, 5, 6, 8 and 16, mark the heart shape on the right side of the fabric and cut out the hearts leaving ¼in allowance.

Turn under the allowance and baste, then baste the heart into position on the background fabric. Appliqué in place with a blind stitch.

BLOCKS

Block 1

Appliqué the hearts in place onto the background.

Block 2

Vliesofix the sunflower to the background and Buttonhole Stitch around all of the shapes.

Block 10

Vliesofix the geese to background and Buttonhole Stitch around the shapes.

Join the 5½in x 1in black strip to the bottom and the same size coloured strip to the top.

Block 11

Join two B pieces to each side of one A piece five times, then join them in rows.

Block 12

For block 12, join the 5½in x 1½in check strip to the 6½in x 1½in strip to the bottom.

Vliesofix the rooster into place and Buttonhole around the shapes.

Block 13

Vliesofix the sunflowers in place and Buttonhole around the shapes.

Block 14

Vliesofix the flowers to the block and Buttonhole around the edges of the flowers. Join the 5½in x 1½in check strip to the top.

Block 15

Appliqué pieces 6 to 5 and 8 to 7 before piecing this block.

Join three lots of two A pieces of different fabrics, then join these three pieced sections into a row.

Join the two sets of pieces 3 and 4 (one in reverse).

Join these two sections to either end of piece 5. Join this pieced section to piece 7.

Join piece 2 to each side, then attach piece 1 along the top.

Finally attach the pieced triangle strip to the top of piece 1.

Block 16

For block 16, appliqué the hearts onto the background fabric using a blind stitch as shown in the photograph on page 60.

ASSEMBLY

Join blocks 1, 2 and 3 and add the 1½in x 9½in check strip to the bottom of the unit. Join this to block 4. Join blocks 5 and 6 and add to block 4.

Join blocks 10 and 14, add to block 11, then join to block 7. Join blocks 8, 12 and 15. Join blocks 9, 13 and 16. Join the 8, 12, 15 unit to the 9, 13, 16 unit. Join the two bottom units, then attach this unit to the top unit.

Add the check inner borders to the top and bottom, press, then add the side borders. For the black outer border, add the side borders first, then add the top and bottom sections.

Layout diagram

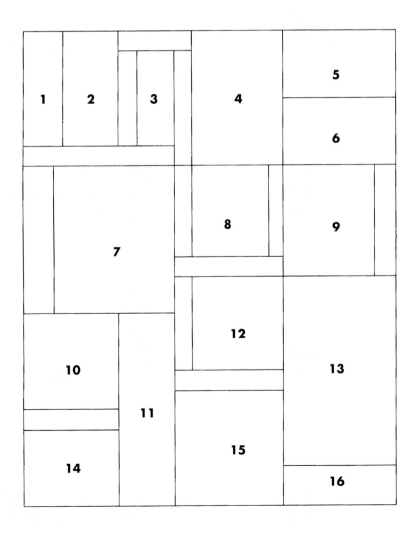

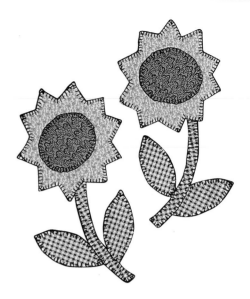

Vliesofix twelve sunflowers around the border, using the photograph as a guide for placement, and Buttonhole Stitch around the edges.

Add the embroidery details, including the girl's face, cows' mouths, the sheep's eyes, the geese eyes, the barn doors and weather vane and the rooster's eye.

QUILTING

Layer the backing, batting and quilt top together and pin or baste through all three layers.

Add buttons, as shown in the photograph, attaching them through all layers.

Using six strands of embroidery thread, tie the quilt at the corner of each block, taking both ends of the thread through to the back and tying them off.

Hand quilt around the stars, sheep, girl, cows, small flowers, barn, hearts and inside the triangles on blocks 11 and 15.

FINISHING

❖

BINDING

Fold the strips in half lengthwise, with wrong sides together and press.

Attach the side strips to the front of the quilt, with all the raw edges together.

Press out, then attach the top and bottom strips in the same manner.

Turn binding to the back and slip stitch in place.

Make a label for the back and sign and date your quilt.

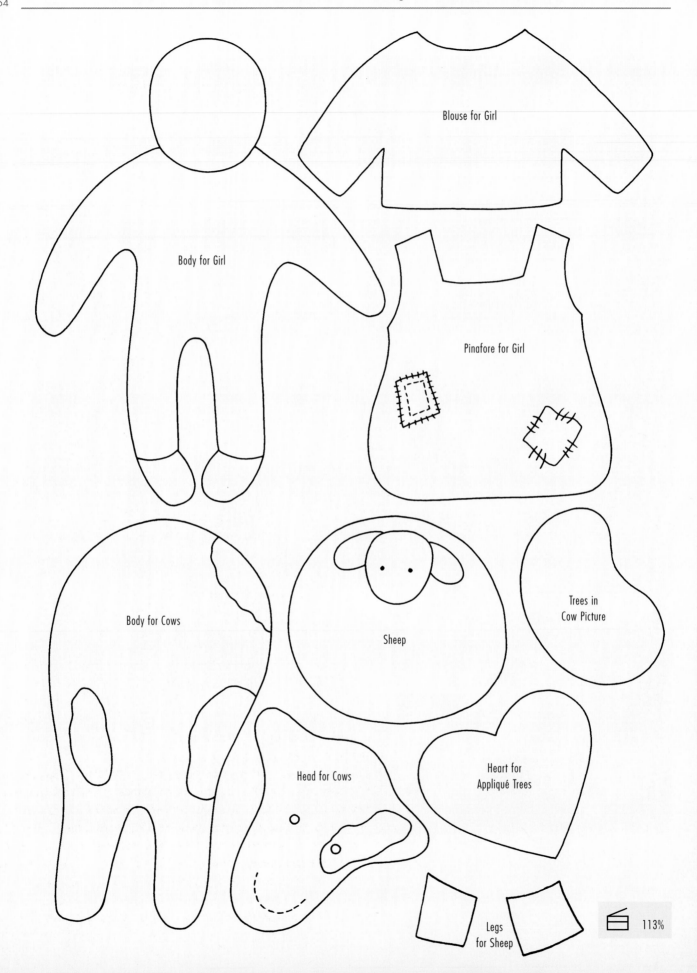

Body for Girl

Blouse for Girl

Pinafore for Girl

Body for Cows

Sheep

Trees in
Cow Picture

Head for Cows

Heart for
Appliqué Trees

Legs
for Sheep

113%

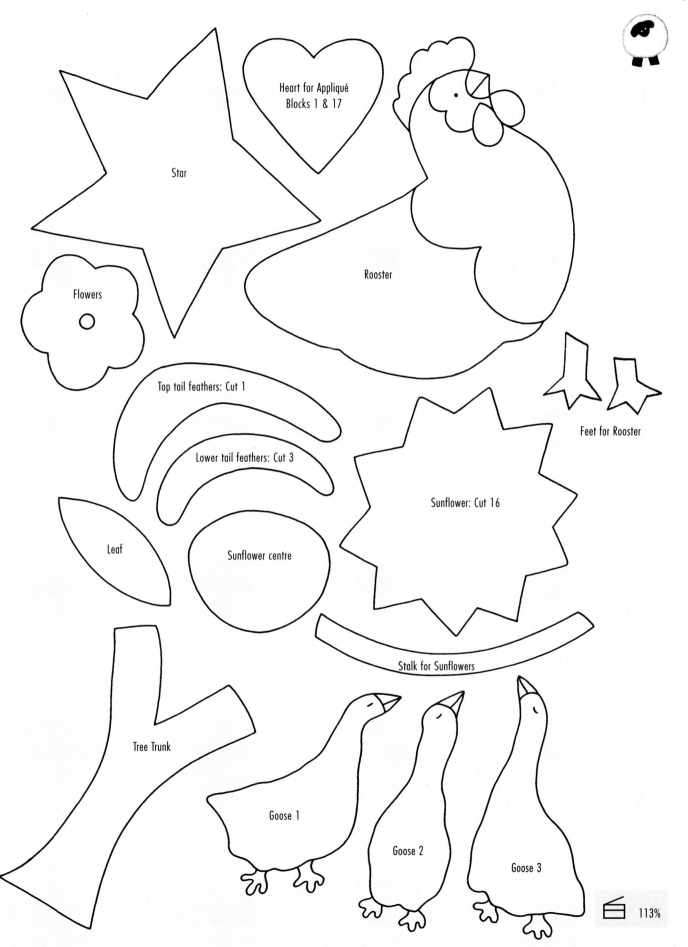

Heart for Appliqué
Blocks 1 & 17

Star

Rooster

Flowers

Feet for Rooster

Top tail feathers: Cut 1

Lower tail feathers: Cut 3

Sunflower: Cut 16

Leaf

Sunflower centre

Stalk for Sunflowers

Tree Trunk

Goose 1

Goose 2

Goose 3

113%

Farmyard Appliqué Quilt

*Plaids, stripes, star and animal prints have been used to quaint effect
in this farmyard quilt. Use some of your favourite crazy fabrics to appliqué
a farmyard scene, then decorate the quilt with colourful buttons. Make
matching cushions or a wall-hanging from your favourite blocks.*

PREPARATION

CUTTING

Wash and iron all fabrics. Cut the background fabric into the following block sizes:

Block 1 wheelbarrows
14cm x 35.5cm

Block 2 five hearts
14cm x 22cm

Block 3 house with three trees
14cm x 33cm

Block 4 scarecrow and turnips
33cm x 30cm

Block 5 two houses and tree
33cm x 12cm

Block 6 six apples
27.5cm x 23cm

Block 7 five hearts
23cm x 14.5cm

Block 8 three pumpkins
12.5cm x 33.5cm

Block 9 sheep in paddock
29cm x 33.5cm

Block 10 pigs and tree
40cm x 22cm

Block 11 six hearts
16cm x 23cm

Block 12 three toadstools
32cm x 9cm

Block 13 five cats
32cm x 13cm

Cut all sashings 5.5cm wide by the length required. The seam allowance through-

out is lcm, which gives leeway for any minor distortions.

The finished size of all blocks and sashings is 2cm less than the cut size.

CONSTRUCTION

Onto the front of each block, rule a pencil line to mark the finished size. This will help in placing the appliquéd shapes and can be used as a stitching guide when adding the sashings.

There are two methods for making this quilt. Make up the whole quilt background and appliqué the shapes on, or appliqué each block and join them together. The second method is perhaps the more manageable.

APPLIQUE

Using the template patterns provided, trace all the farm shapes onto thin cardboard. Trace out as many shapes as necessary following the quilt layout diagram.

Cut out the fabrics of your choice for each shape leaving 5mm seam allowance. Baste the fabric onto the right side of each cardboard shape using strong cotton. Do not nick the corners until you have stitched up to them, as the fabric can distort while you are basting.

Once the pieces of card have been covered, press them on the back and front with a warm iron to make a firm fold. Leave the cardboard in each shape until you are ready to appliqué it. Give the shape a final press before removing the basting stitches and card. Re-baste the shape into position on the background block and appliqué around the edges with matching thread to hold the shape in position. Continue pressing and tacking in this way for all shapes until each block has been completed.

When positioning the shapes ready to appliqué them onto the quilt, make sure

FINISHED SIZE

- 114cm x 123cm (45in x 48½in)

MATERIALS

- 1.5m (1¾yd) light-coloured background fabric
- 40cm (½yd) each of two dark fabrics for the checkerboard sashing
- 50cm (⅔yd) fabric for the outer border
- 60cm (⅔yd) fabric for the binding
- 1.3m (1½yd) backing fabric
- 1.3m (1½yd) batting
- 20cm (¼yd) each of fifteen assorted prints for the appliqué and sashings
- 30 assorted coloured buttons
- 25cm (10in) flat embroidered cord for the scarecrow
- 25cm (10in) glazed embroidered cord for the pigs' tails
- 2 sheets of thin cardboard
- 2B pencil
- Sewing cotton to match fabrics
- Sharp needles
- 30 small black beads for eyes
- Rotary cutter and scissors

NOTE: This project has been designed using metric measurements.

Step 1
Use checks and novelty prints for the appliqué shapes.

Step 2
Baste the fabric onto cardboard shapes and press well with an iron.

Diagram 1

SASHINGS

Join the completed blocks together with the sashings following the numerical sequence set out on the block assembly diagram. Refer to the coloured photograph of the finished quilt for further guidance if required.

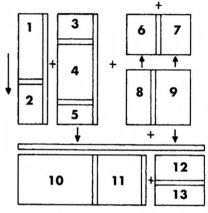

Block assembly diagram

CHECKERBOARD SASHING

When all the blocks are joined together, attach the inner checkered border. To make this border, cut five strips of each of two contrasting fabrics. These strips should be 3cm x 115cm each. Alternating the fabrics, sew the strips together lengthwise using a 5mm seam. Press all seams towards the darker fabric.

Cut the sheet that you have just made into thirds across its length and resew the thirds together to make one long striped

that the necessary edges are concealed under the top shapes where appropriate. For example, the lower edges of the chimneys are concealed under the roof and the top edge of the main body of the house under the lower edge of the roof. Similarly, the tree foliage should overlap the top edge of the trunks and the scarecrow's arms should be placed slightly under the body.

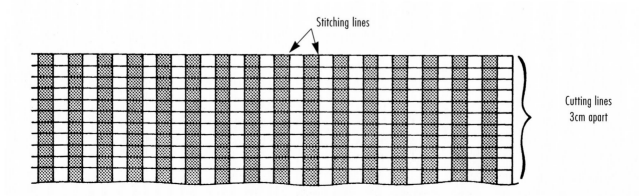

Stitching lines

Cutting lines
3cm apart

piece. Make sure that the fabrics continue to alternate.

Use a rotary cutter to cut 3cm wide strips across this piece (see Diagram 1). Sew pairs of these strips together to make a set of checkered strips.

Machine these border strips around the completed quilt top. Continue the checkerboard effect around each corner, and add to the cut strips if you find they are not long enough.

EMBELLISHMENTS

Sew the small black beads as eyes onto the scarecrow, sheep, pigs and cats. Attach the flat embroidered cord for the scarecrow's pole.

Use the glazed embroidered cord, twisted into shape, to make the pigs' tails.

OUTER BORDER

Cut four strips of fabric 11cm x 115cm. Using a 5mm seam allowance, sew strips across the top and bottom of the quilt, then down each side.

Press all the seams. Sandwich the layers of the quilt together, placing the batting between the quilt top and the backing fabric. Pin the three layers together or baste them by hand in a zigzag fashion.

Work from the centre to the outside edges. This will hold the quilt together while the binding and buttons are being sewn on.

Remove the tacking when the quilt is completed.

FINISHING

BINDING

Cut four 14cm wide strips for the binding. Fold these strips in half, wrong sides together, and press.

Pin one strip to the right side of the top and to the bottom edges of the quilt.

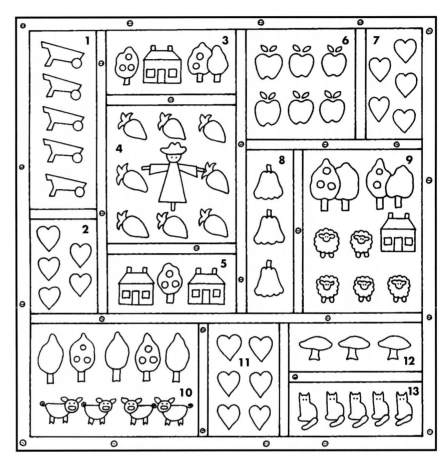

Quilt layout diagram.
⊙ *Button placement.*

Machine stitch the binding right around the quilt.

Trim the quilt and batting to 2cm from the machine line of the binding. Turn the binding over to the wrong side and slip stitch into place. Repeat these steps to attach the binding along the side edges of the quilt.

If you plan to use your quilt as a wall-hanging, attach a sleeve to the wrong side of the quilt, just below the binding, and insert a rod.

Sew the assorted coloured buttons onto the quilt at the places as marked on the quilt layout diagram. Sew through all three layers of the quilt to hold it firmly together.

Any extra hand or machine quilting can also be added at this time if you wish.

Make a label for the back of your quilt and sign and date it.

This happy quilt is sure to be a favourite with all the family.

111%

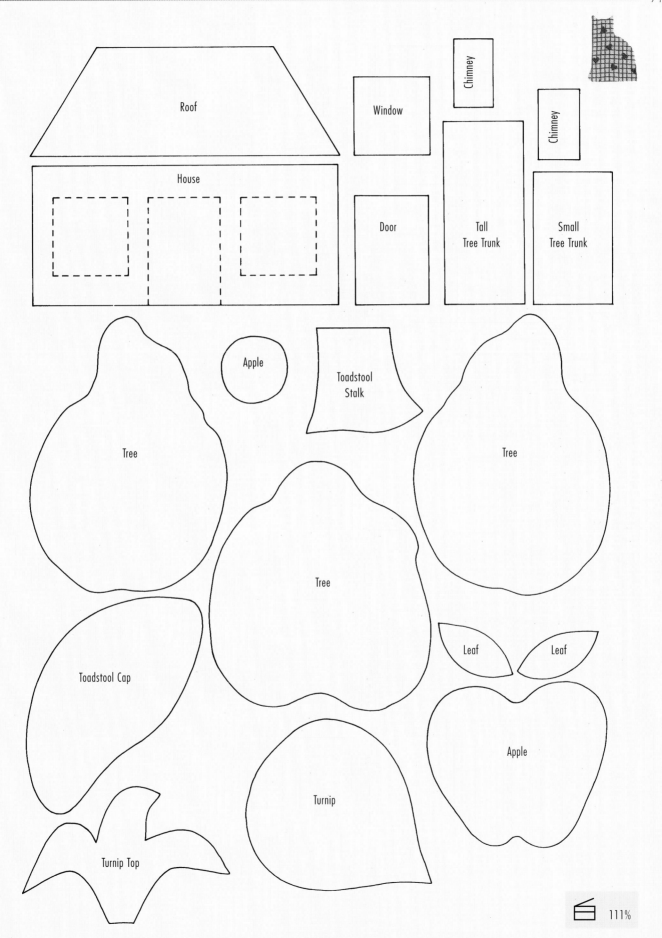

Roof

Window

Chimney

Chimney

House

Door

Tall
Tree Trunk

Small
Tree Trunk

Apple

Toadstool
Stalk

Tree

Tree

Tree

Toadstool Cap

Leaf

Leaf

Apple

Turnip

Turnip Top

111%

Naive Dove Cushion

This soft and serene original dove design
can be either stitched onto a purchased cushion cover,
or you can choose your own background fabric
and frame it.

PREPARATION

Mark the centre of your fabric and trace the pattern onto the cushion or the background fabric using a water-erasable blue pen.

CONSTRUCTION

EMBROIDERY

Work the tree using three strands of embroidery thread in your chosen colour. Use Stem Stitch for the trunk of the tree and Fern Stitch for the tree branches. Work each of the flower buds with Satin Stitch. Work a Lazy Daisy leaf each side of the buds.

You will find instructions for the embroidery stitches on page 74.

APPLIQUE

Make paper templates by tracing the shapes of the bird onto lightweight cardboard. Cut them out carefully. Place the cardboard shape on the wrong side of the chosen fabric and pin it in place. Cut out around the shape, adding ¼in seam allowance as you cut.

Fold the seam allowance firmly to the back of the template and baste it in place through the cardboard. Ensure that you have a smooth edge. You may need to clip the curves and make small tucks on the wrong side to ease the fullness as you baste it to the cardboard.

Press the work well, with the cardboard inserted, and use spray starch if necessary to achieve a crisp edge. Do not remove the cardboard until you are ready to appliqué the embroidered piece to the background. Remove the basting and ease the cardboard out carefully so as not to disturb the shape.

FINISHED SIZE

• 51cm (20in) square

MATERIALS

• Small amounts of fabric in three colours for bird appliqué

• Matching thread for appliqué

• Stranded embroidery threads for tree and bird detail

• Purchased cushion cover, or, if you wish to frame it, a 51cm (20in) square piece of background fabric

• Lightweight cardboard for templates and appliqué

• 8 small buttons

• Water-erasable blue pen

• Spray starch

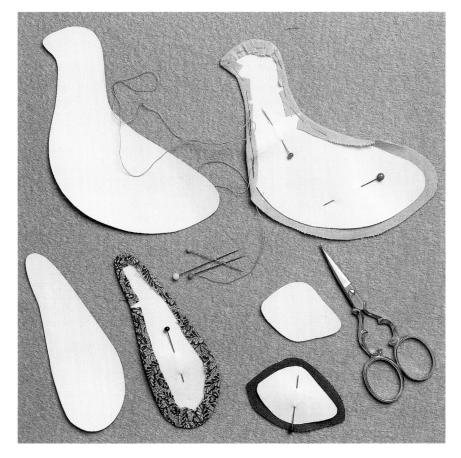

Fold the seam allowance firmly to the back of the cardboard template and baste it in place through the cardboard.

Position and pin the shapes on the cushion or background and using a small hidden slip stitch, showing as little thread as possible, appliqué to the background.

It is important to match your thread as closely as possible to the fabric piece you are appliquéing.

NOTE: The cardboard templates will need to be reversed for the second bird to face the other way.

FINISHING

❖

To finish your cushion or wall-hanging, embroider the birds' legs and beaks in Stem Stitch, again using three strands of the embroidery thread, and attach the eight small buttons as shown in the photograph, using coordinating threads.

Outline the birds' legs and feet with the embroidery thread using a small running stitch.

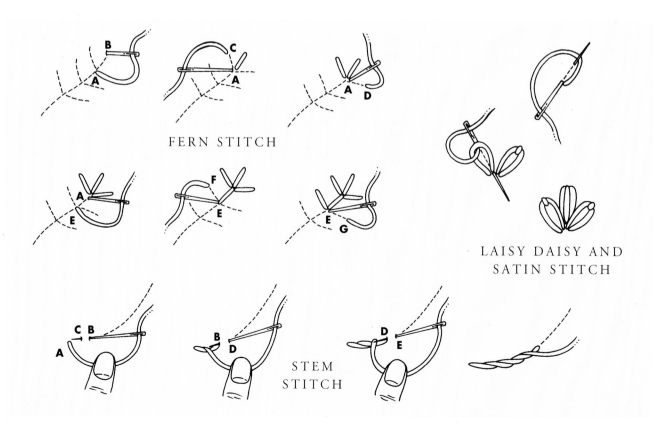

FERN STITCH

LAISY DAISY AND
SATIN STITCH

STEM
STITCH

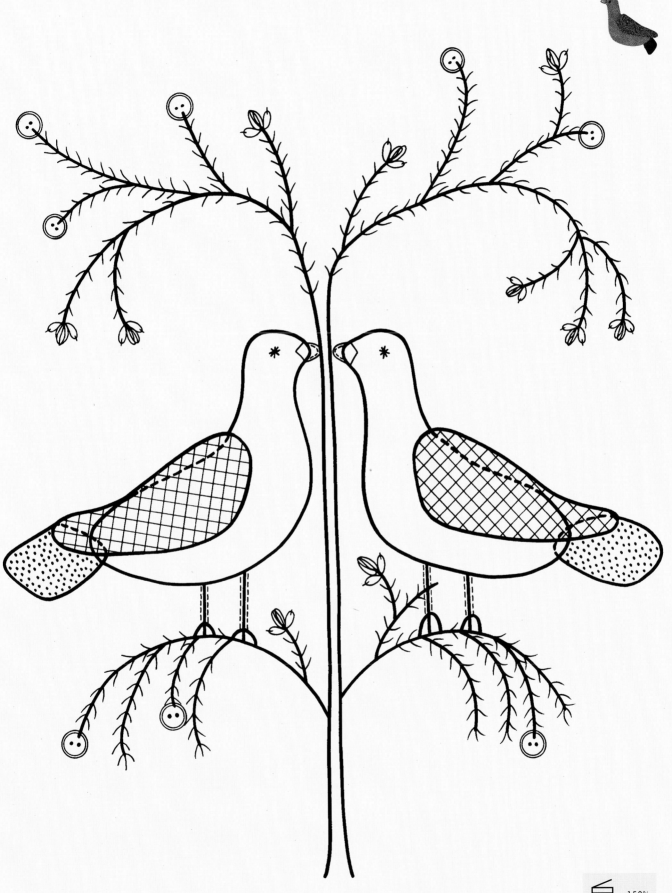

Classical Cats

*Classical Cats is the perfect name for this striking quilt
covered with cute cats made in assorted tartans on
a cream background. The blocks are pulled together
with a different tartan sashing.*

PREPARATION

CUTTING

Assorted tartans

Cut one 2½in square and one 5½in x 4½in rectangle for each cat. There are twelve cats in total.

Black homespun

Cut two strips 1in wide. Cross-cut these strips into 48 x 1in squares to use for the cats' ears.

Cut the remaining black homespun on the bias for the tails.

Cut twelve strips, 1¼in x 6in on the bias.

Cream print fabric

Cut the following strips as in the block diagram. (It's a good idea to keep each set of strips separate and numbered.)

1 Cut one strip 3¾in wide. Cross-cut this strip into twelve 1¾in rectangles.

2 Cut one strip 1¼in wide. Cross-cut this strip into twelve 2½in rectangles.

3 Cut one strip 1in wide. Cross-cut this strip into twelve 2½in rectangles.

4 Cut one strip 5¼in wide. Cross-cut this strip into twelve 3¾in rectangles.

5 Cut one strip 5¼in wide. Cross-cut this strip into twelve 2¼in rectangles.

6 Cut two strips 1¼in wide. Cross-cut this strip into twelve 5½in rectangles.

7 Cut one strip 5¼in wide. Cross-cut this strip into twelve 1¾in rectangles.

From scraps of the leftover strips, cut twenty-four 1in pieces for the cats' chins. Cut twelve 1¼in squares for the backs.

From the red binding fabric cut five strips 2¼in wide.

PIECING

Upper ears

With right sides together, diagonally stitch a black 1in square to the lower corners of a 1in x 2½in rectangle (No 3 in the cream print fabric). Trim the black fabric and press the triangles back across the corners (see step 1 and diagram).

Lower ears and face shape

With right sides together, diagonally stitch a black 1in square to the upper corners of the 2½in tartan squares (see step 1, 2 and diagram). Trim and press back as in step 1.

With right sides together, diagonally stitch a 1in square of cream print fabric to the lower corners of the same tartan square. Trim and press back.

Matching the black ears and with right sides together, stitch the upper ears to the lower ears and face.

With right sides together, join a 1¼in x 2½in rectangle (No 2) to the upper edge of the completed face.

Join a 1¾in x 3¾in rectangle (No 1) to the left side of the cat's face.

Join a 3¾in x 5¼in rectangle (No 4) to the right side of the cat's face.

With right sides together, diagonally stitch a 1¼in cream square to the upper right corner of 4½in x 5½in tartan body rectangle. Trim the seam allowance and press back. This defines the cat's back.

Join a rectangle (No 6), 1¼in x 5½in to the lower edge of the cat's body.

To make the tail, fold the black bias strip in half lengthwise with wrong sides together. Stitch the raw edges together. Insert a ¼in bias bar into the tube, rolling the seam allowance so that it sits flat along the centre of the back. Press in one direction ensuring that the open back seam sits flat. Remove the bias bar. The bias strip can now be curved with the aid of an iron.

Baste tail to the lower corner of the cat's body. Join a 1¾in x 5¼in rectangle (No 7) to the right side of the body.

FINISHED SIZE

- 36in x 46in (91.5cm x 117cm)
- Block size 20cm (8in)

MATERIALS

- Assorted tartan scraps for the cats, or purchase 15cm (¼yd) of each tartan fabric
- 15cm (¼yd) black homespun
- 65cm (¾yd) tartan for sashings
- 1m (1⅛yd) cream print for background and borders
- 1.3m (1½yd) backing fabric
- Batting to fit
- Rotary cutter, ruler and mat
- Neutral thread
- Black thread
- Set of bias pressing bars
- Sewing machine and general sewing supplies
- Thread for quilting

NOTE: 6mm (¼in) seam allowance is used throughout.

Step 1
Attach 2.5cm (1in) black squares to corners of the rectangle, trim and fold back to make the ear section.

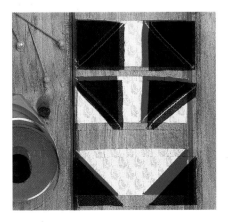

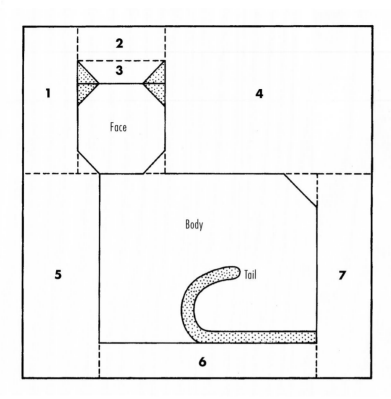

Layout diagram for completed Cat Block.

Step 2

Create the face shape by attaching squares to the corners of the main cat fabric square.

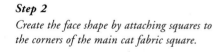

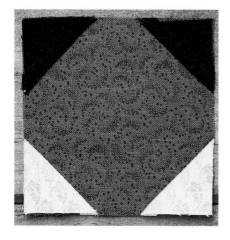

Join a 2¼in x 5½in rectangle (No 5) to the left side of the body.

Press both sections of the cat block. With right sides facing, stitch both sections of the block together being careful to align the cat's chin with the body of the cat. Press the completed block.

Curve the tail as desired and invisibly slip stitch into place.

Make another eleven Cat Blocks.

SASHING

From the tartan fabric cut four sashing strips 2½in wide. Cross-cut into sixteen 8½in strips. Try to match the tartan pattern in each strip.

Using the colour photograph as a guide, stitch the sashing strips to the sides of the blocks, joining the three blocks together per row. Complete four rows of blocks.

Measure the width of the rows of blocks, approximately 32½in. Cut five strips 2½in wide by the measured width. Stitch these sashing strips across the top of four rows of blocks and one across the lower edge of the last row.

Join the rows together and press.

BORDERS

Measure the length of the quilt top through the centre of the quilt. From the cream print fabric cut two border strips 2½in wide to equal this measurement and sew them to the sides of the quilt. Press the seams out.

Measure the width across the centre of the quilt and cut and add 2½in borders to the upper and lower edges. Press the seams out.

Layer the quilt top, batting and backing. Baste the three layers together. Quilt by hand or machine as desired. Our cat quilt is quilted in the ditch around each cat shape, the background area of each block is stipple quilted and there are parallel rows of straight stitching along the tartan sashing strips and outer border.

FINISHING

❖

BINDING

Join the five 2¼in binding strips together using 45 degree angled seams. Press the strip in half lengthwise with the wrong sides together.

With all raw edges together, attach the binding to the front of the quilt using a ¼in seam allowance. Trim any excess batting and backing.

Roll the binding to the quilt back and firmly hand stitch in place.

Don't forget to label and date the back of your quilt.

Golden Fleece

Crazy piecing forms the centre panel of this cosy quilt, with images of sheep, shearing and the outback appliquéd to the borders. Although not for the beginner, some of the blocks and appliqué images could be used to make a small wall-hanging or cushion.

PREPARATION

Aged woollen clothing and blankets have been recycled to make this warm and cosy woollen quilt.

If you have purchased any woollen garments from a second-hand shop, machine wash them using a normal cold cycle, then line dry. This removes any op-shop odours and slightly 'felts' the wool. Discard any skirts that don't stand up to this treatment. Handwash new wool fabrics in warm water.

Remove buttons, zips, waistbands and linings and lightly press the fabric using a steam iron on wool setting.

Using a rotary cutter, ruler and mat, cut pieces of each woollen skirt into strips. Cut them wedge-shaped, straight, thick and thin pieces, varying in width from 1in to 3in.

CONSTRUCTION

CRAZY PATCH BLOCKS

Using a piece of bright flannel approximately 2in x 3in for the centre of each block, add strips of fabric in Log Cabin style until the block measures more than 8in square. Press the seams open as you progress using a steam iron on wool setting. Be careful not to scorch the wool. Select your strips in a random fashion so that every block is different. Make thirty blocks in this manner.

Using a ruler and rotary cutter, trim the blocks to 8in square. Move the blocks around in a 5 x 6 grid until you find a pleasing arrangement. Join five blocks together to make a row. Make six rows each of five blocks. To make the quilt centre, join the rows together, taking care

FINISHED SIZE

- 127cm x 147.5cm (50in x 58in)
- Block size 19cm (7½in)

MATERIALS

- Various wool and wool blend fabrics with at least 70 per cent wool content. (Nine different coloured skirts were used in this project.)
- Old grey blanket or 1m x 1.5m (40in x 60in) grey wool for borders
- 30cm (⅓yd) bright flannel shirting for the centre of the blocks
- Extra skirts for backing
- 140cm x 160cm (55in x 63in) wool batting
- 60cm (⅔yd) Vliesofix fusible webbing
- Sewing threads to match appliqué images
- Rotary cutter, cutting mat, ruler
- Chenille sewing needles for quilting
- Coton Perlé No 5 for quilting (three skeins of grey, some red and black)
- Open-toed embroidery foot
- Walking foot

NOTE: 6mm (¼in) seam allowance is used throughout.

Step 1
Wool strips ready to sew Log Cabin style.

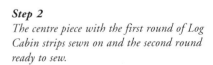

Step 2
The centre piece with the first round of Log Cabin strips sewn on and the second round ready to sew.

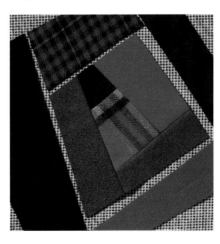

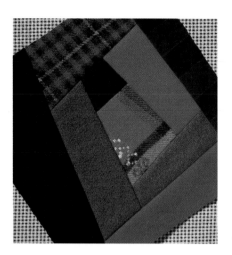

Step 3
The completed block trimmed to 8in.

to match the corners. Press the seams open. The quilt should now measure approximately 37¾in x 45¾in.

APPLIQUE

The appliqué shapes are on the Pattern Sheet. Trace the appliqué shapes onto the paper side of the Vliesofix and cut them out just slightly beyond the line of the pencil. You will note that one of the shearers is reversed, one of the sheep is used twice and there are two different windmill shapes. You will need three kangaroos and seven fence posts. Select the fabrics for these shapes.

For this project we have used plain weaves and felt pieces in browns and red.

Press the scraps onto the wrong side of the wool fabrics using a dry iron. Cut them to shape along the pencil line using sharp scissors and the Vliesofix peel-away paper backing.

You will not require a seam allowance because each of the appliquéd shapes is attached to the border using a zigzag stitch on the machine.

BORDERS

Measure lengthwise through the centre of the quilt to obtain the required length of the side borders approximately 45¾in. Cut strips to this size from a grey blanket 7½in wide. Using the photograph of the quilt as a guide, position the appliqué shapes in the centre of the side border strips. Note that there is a small and large windmill – the larger windmill is used on the side border and the smaller windmill is positioned on the top border. Press and machine-stitch into place using a small zigzag stitch (width 2.5, length 1.0) on the edge of each shape. The webbing and the wool don't fuse together well, but the appliqué will stay in place long enough to stitch down. Match the cotton to the colour of each appliqué shape and loosen the top tension slightly. An open-toed embroidery foot allows you to see clearly. Pin and stitch the side border strips to both sides of the quilt. Press the seams open.

Cut border strips for the top and bottom of the quilt 7½in wide and the

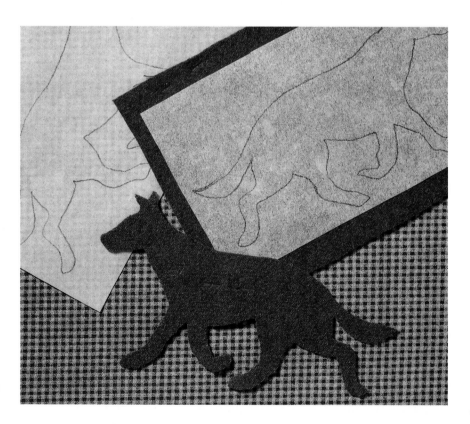

Step 4
Trace the appliqué shapes onto Vliesofix, iron onto fabric piece and cut to shape.

length of the pieced centre plus the side borders approximately 51in. Using the picture of the quilt as a guide, position the remaining appliqué shapes, press and machine stitch as above. The barbed wire fence is an asterisk stitch and a straight stitch on a sewing machine, but it can be worked by hand.

When the appliqué is complete, pin and stitch the borders to the top and bottom of the quilt.

BACKING

Using large pieces of wool fabric from two more skirts and scraps from the front of the quilt, piece together a backing to fit the quilt top. Add some leftover appliqué shapes for interest if you wish.

QUILTING

The 'inside-out' method has been used to join the quilt together. Make sure the top of the quilt is perfectly square by measuring and trimming to size, then layer batting and backing right side up, and the top of the quilt right side down. Smooth and pin carefully around the edge. Leaving a gap large enough to turn the quilt through, sew around all sides using a ¼in seam allowance. Trim away excess batting and backing and clip corners. Turn through and hand stitch the opening closed. Using the walking foot, stitch around the edge of the quilt again using a ¼in seam allowance.

This method requires a great deal of care for a quilt this size so you may wish to finish the quilt in the traditional manner using a binding.

FINISHING

❖

When you have finished the quilting, use a large quilting stitch to gather the edges of the quilt slightly and use a Coton Perlé over the top of the machine stitching to

prevent fluting. Smooth out the quilt, to flatten it, then pin it with safety pins approximately 4in apart. Machine quilt in the ditch around the borders and around each of the centre blocks of the quilt.

Using the grey, red and black Coton Perlé, quilt in slightly wavy lines across the entire top of the quilt and through the borders in both directions. Alternatively, you could tie the quilt if you wish to do so.

A dark line of stitching has also been used around both sides of the borders.

If you wish, you can make your quilt into a wall-hanging by adding a rod pocket.

Now, label and date your quilt.

Baa Baa Plaid Sheep

This small country-style Australian quilt depicts a mob of sheep on a distant hill. Simple to make, it features an easy strip-cutting construction method. Make the sheep in an assortment of plaid fabrics or put your imagination to the test with your own selection of fabrics.

PREPARATION

Please read the entire instructions carefully before proceeding. All fabric requirements are given for 100 per cent cotton fabric, 115cm (45in) wide. Wash and iron all fabrics beforehand. With 100 per cent cotton fabrics, it is a good idea to dry each piece of fabric until just damp and then iron them.

The sheep blocks are created by rows, as indicated in Diagram 1. Note that rows 1 and 8 and rows 2 and 7 are identical. Rows 3 and 6 are a mirror image of each other and rows 4/5 are really just one row of double width. These rows will be referred to in both the cutting and in the assembly instructions.

NOTE: Measurements given throughout the pattern include seam allowances.

CUTTING

Rows 1 and 8

Cut two strips of calico $3\frac{1}{2}$in wide across the width of the fabric.

From the navy fabric, cut two strips $3\frac{1}{2}$in wide and two strips $2\frac{1}{2}$in wide, also across the width.

Rows 2 and 7

From the calico, cut two strips $5\frac{1}{2}$in wide. From the navy fabric, cut two strips $2\frac{1}{2}$in wide and two strips $1\frac{1}{2}$in wide.

Rows 3 and 6

Cut two strips of calico $3\frac{1}{2}$in wide. Cross-cut those strips into fifty units, each $1\frac{1}{2}$in. Cut two strips of calico $4\frac{1}{2}$in wide. Cross-cut those strips into fifty units each $1\frac{1}{2}$in.

Row 4/5

Cut four strips of calico $2\frac{1}{2}$in wide. Cross-cut two of those strips to make twenty-five squares, each $2\frac{1}{2}$in. Leave the remaining two strips uncut.

Cut two more strips of calico $1\frac{3}{8}$in wide. Cross-cut these strips into fifty squares, each $1\frac{3}{8}$in.

From the navy fabric, cut two strips $1\frac{1}{2}$in wide.

The sheep

From the assorted plaid fabrics, cut the following for each of the twenty-five sheep. Cut four $1\frac{1}{2}$in squares and one $2\frac{1}{2}$in x $3\frac{1}{2}$in rectangle.

Cut the sashings, borders and bias binding from the remaining length of navy fabric. The sashing and borders should be cut parallel to the selvedge.

The selvedge should not be used in any of the quilt pieces. Make sure you remove it before you begin cutting. See Diagram 2 for the cutting layout – this includes the sashing, two side borders, the top and bottom borders and the bias binding.

FINISHED SIZE

- 146cm (57$\frac{1}{2}$in square)
- Block size 20cm (8in)

MATERIALS

- 1.6m (1$\frac{3}{4}$yd) calico
- 2.6m (3yd) navy fabric (for quilt top, borders and bias binding)
- Five or more fat eighths of assorted plaids will make up to five sheep. **NOTE:** The more plaids you choose, the more variety in your 'mob'.
- 2.5m (2$\frac{3}{4}$yd) backing fabric
- 1.6m (1$\frac{3}{4}$yd) square piece of thin batting
- Sewing machine (6mm (1/4in) foot designed for your machine is a big asset for accuracy)
- Rotary cutter, ruler and mat
- New No 70 or 80 universal machine needle
- 100 per cent cotton machine thread
- Quilting thread in cream and navy

Diagram 2
Cutting layout for the sashings, borders and bias binding.

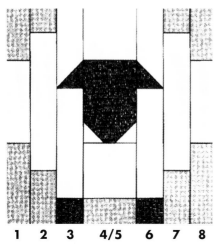

Diagram 1 The sheep block is created in rows.

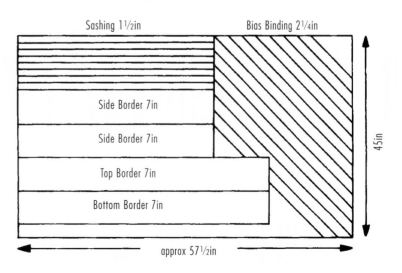

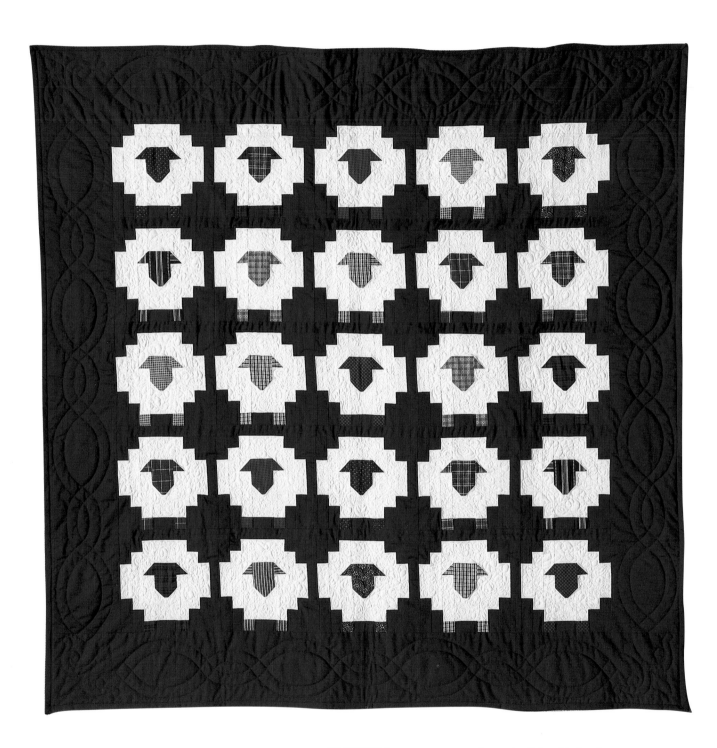

SASHINGS

Cutting parallel to the selvedge, cut eight strips 44½in x 1½in from the navy fabric for the sashings. Cross-cut four of those strips into sixteen lengths, each 8½in.

BORDERS

Again, cutting parallel to the selvedge, cut two strips of the navy fabric, 44½in x 7in for each of the side borders.

Cut two strips of fabric, 57½in x 7in for the top and bottom borders.

BIAS BINDING

After you have cut out the sashings and borders, there should be enough of the remaining navy fabric to cut enough strips to measure approximately 260in x 2¼in for the bias binding.

CONSTRUCTION

BLOCK ASSEMBLY

NOTE: All seam allowances measure an exact ¼in.

Rows 1 and 8

Sew a 3½in navy strip and a 2½in navy strip to each of the 3½in calico strips. Press all the seam allowances toward the navy fabric.

Cross-cut these sewn strips into fifty sections, each 1½in (see Diagram 3).

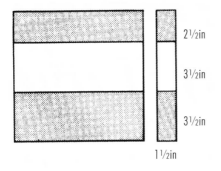

Diagram 3
Rows 1 and 8.
Sew the strips and cross-cut into fifty sections each 1½in.

Rows 2 and 7

Sew a 2½in navy strip and a 1½in navy strip to each of the 5½in calico strips. Press seam allowances toward the navy strips. Cross-cut these sewn strips into fifty sections, each 1½in (see Diagram 4).

Rows 3 and 6

Use the fifty calico pieces (3½in x 1½in), the fifty calico pieces (4½in x 1½in) and the one hundred 1½in plaid squares.

To each 4½in x 1½in calico piece, sew a 1½in plaid square as shown in the step-by-step photograph. Press the seam allowance toward the calico.

To each of the 3½in x 1½in calico pieces, sew a 1½in plaid square on the diagonal. Make sure that you have equal numbers, with the diagonal in opposite directions. See the photograph for details and sew twenty-five A pieces and twenty-five B pieces.

Trim the seam allowance to ⅛in and press the seam allowance towards the plaid fabric. Construct rows 3 and 6 as shown in the photograph.

Press the joining seam allowance towards the calico.

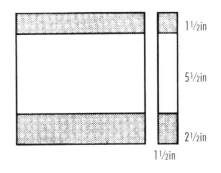

Diagram 4
Rows 2 and 7.
Sew the strips and cross-cut into fifty sections each 1½in.

Rows 3 and 6.
Sew a 4½in x 1½in calico piece to a 1½in plaid square across the diagonal of the square to make sections A and B (1).
Sew a 3½in x 1½in calico piece to a 1½in plaid square (2). Sew the two sections together to make each row.

Row 4/5.
Sew a navy strip to each of the two calico strips, then cross-cut into 2½in sections. Place a 1⅜in calico square on the corner of each of the plaid rectangles and sew diagonally across the calico, corner to corner.

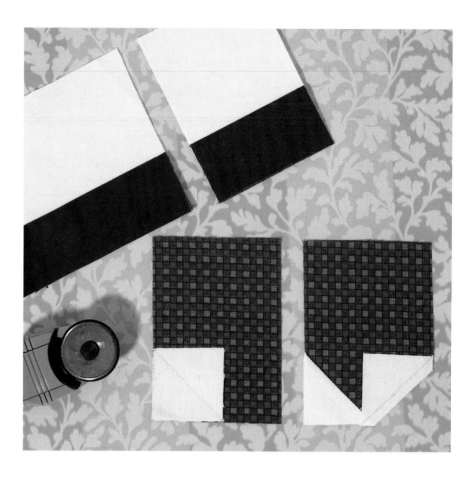

Row 4/5

To each of the two 2½in calico strips, sew a 1½in navy strip. Press the seam allowance toward the navy. Cross-cut these sewn strips into twenty-five sections, each 2½in (see photograph above). To each of the twenty-five plaid rectangles 2½in x 3½in place a 1⅜in calico square on the corner as shown in the photograph. Sew diagonally across the calico, corner to corner. Trim to a ⅛in seam allowance and finger-press open. Add a second calico square on the opposite corner in the same manner.

Construct row 4/5 referring to Diagram 1. Press seam allowances toward the calico.

To create each block, refer to Diagram 1. Be sure to line up the top of the head and the ears when sewing together. Press the seam allowances toward the outside edges from the centre. Make twenty-five sheep blocks.

SASHING

Lay out the blocks five across and five down so that you get the desired arrangement of plaids. Using the 8½in x 1½in lengths of navy, join the blocks in horizontal rows. Press the seam allowance toward the sashing.

Join the rows together using the 44½in x 1½in navy strips. Press them towards the sashing. Be sure to keep the vertical elements (blocks and sashing) lined up as you join the rows together.

BORDERS

Pin the borders onto the sides of the quilt, easing any fullness that appears in the quilt or border. Now sew the quilt and border together and press towards the border. Pin the top and bottom borders to the quilt top, again easing any fullness as you go.

Machine sew together and press toward the borders.

BACKING

Cut a 33in piece from the backing fabric, (cut across the fabric, selvedge to selvedge). Then, cutting parallel to the selvedge, cut that piece in half. Stitch the backing fabric together as shown in Diagram 5 to make a piece that is large enough for the quilt top. Layer the backing fabric, the batting (both slightly larger than the quilt top) and the quilt top and pin or baste together, working from the centre out.

QUILTING

This quilt has been machine quilted. The outline quilting was done first around each sheep, then a 'wool' pattern was created with free-motion stitching. The outline stitching is necessary to keep the quilt from drawing up when heavy free-motion work is done.

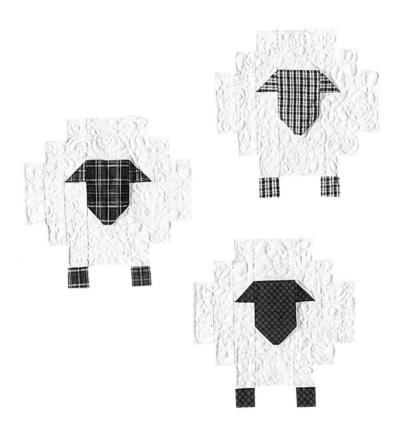

Diagram 5
Piecing the backing fabric.

FINISHING

Binding

Join the bias strips together. Sew the unfolded bias to the top of the quilt using a ½in seam allowance, mitring the corners. Trim away the excess batting and backing fabric.

Turn the binding to the back of the quilt and finish it by hand, using a blind stitch.

NOTE: If you wish to make a single-bed sized quilt, use twenty-four blocks instead of fifty. Arrange them so that there are four blocks across the top of the quilt and six blocks down.

You will also need to adjust the sashing, border, batting and the backing measurements to fit.

For a completely different look, use bold coloured fabrics for the sheep on a white background, and use tartan for the quilt top, borders and binding.

Sign and date your quilt.

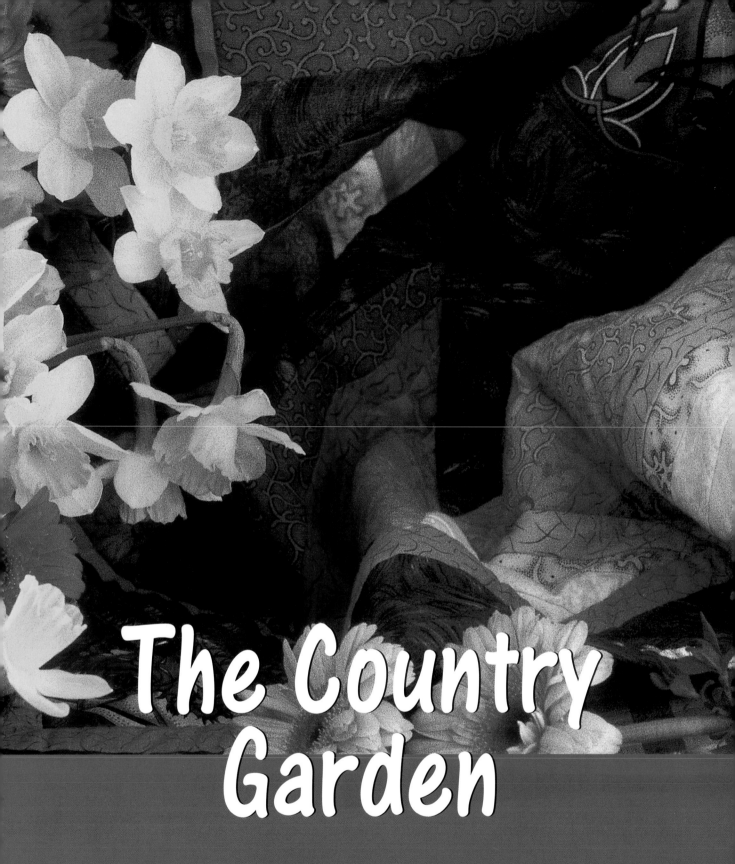

The Country Garden

Flowers are the most commonly used motif in old-fashioned and modern decor. The mere presence of plants and flowers enhances our wellbeing. In fact, almost every flower has been brought to life in the beauty of a quilt. Simple and unsophisticated shapes, reminiscent of a child's drawing contrast with traditional country designs.

Sunbonnet Sue ...
Gardening in the Thirties

This small wall quilt features a traditional 1930s Sunbonnet Sue Block, appliquéd in a range of reproduction fabrics. Featured in her beautiful garden, Sue is surrounded by a white picket fence and appliquéd butterflies.

PREPARATION

CUTTING

From the white background print, cut an 8½in square. Cut four 8½in x 1¾in strips and four 1¾in squares from the various scraps. Sew the strips to the top and bottom of the centre square. Sew a small square to both ends of the remaining two strips. Add the strips, with the squares attached, to either side of the centre square, taking care to match the corners. Again, from the white background print, cut four strips 3½in x 18in. Add these to each side of the centre square, mitring the corners at the same time.

From the green 1930s print fabric, cut four strips 1¼in x 18in long. Add one strip to the top and bottom at the pieced centre, press, then add the remaining two strips to the sides of the centre square. Measure your patchwork now to ensure that it measures 18½in square.

CONSTRUCTION

APPLIQUE AND EMBROIDERY

This appliqué is worked over cardboard templates. Cut accurate templates of each shape from the designs provided and cover them with the chosen fabric, basting the fabric in place. Use a ⅛in to ¼in seam allowance, depending on the size of the piece. Be sure to clip the curves to ensure that the fabric covers the template accurately. Pin the covered template in place and attach it using a matching thread and a small blind stitch. It is important to use a fine needle for accurate appliqué. Remove the tacking and the cardboard from the shape before completing the stitching.

Sunbonnet Sue is appliquéd into position following the number sequence 1 to 12 on the pattern. It was traditional in the 1930s to outline stitch appliqué

with a black line. The stitching around Sunbonnet Sue is worked in two strands of embroidery thread using a Stem Stitch. The flower has embroidered details worked in back stitch and four strands of embroidery thread.

Appliqué the garden into position. Before beginning the floral appliqués, embroider the vine that connects the flowers using green Coton Perlé embroidery thread. This is worked in a large back stitch. Once the vine is in place, appliqué the flowers and leaves, adding the embroidered details last. The oval flowers have their detail worked in six strands of embroidery thread using Stem Stitch. The daisy-like flowers have details worked in the centre oval using six strands and back stitch. All the leaves have a central vein worked in six strands of green thread using a large back stitch.

Picket fence border

The picket fence border is made by piecing two blocks together. Block A is the white pointed picket and Block B is the alternate block that represents the runs of the fence.

The border requires twenty-four A Blocks. From the white on cream stripe fabric, cut twenty-four rectangles 2in x 4½in. From the small green check fabric, cut forty-eight 1⅝in squares. On the reverse of the green squares, using a fine pencil, draw a diagonal line from corner to corner. With right sides together, place a green square on the top left-hand corner of a white picket. Stitch on the drawn diagonal line. Trim back the seam allowance and fold back the corner triangle.

Join another green square to the other side of the top of the white picket in the same manner. Press (see Diagram 1).

For the border you will need twenty-eight B Blocks. Cut three strips across the width of the green check fabric. Cut one strip 2in wide, cut the second strip 1in

FINISHED SIZE

- approximately 66cm (26in) square

MATERIALS

- 60cm (⅔yd) white on white print for the background
- Scraps of the 1930s style prints in green, pink, lavender, yellow and blue
- Background of picket fence: 30cm (⅓yd) small green check
- Fence pickets: 20cm (¼yd) white on cream stripe fabric
- Runs in picket fence: 15cm (¼yd) cream and white ticking stripe fabric
- 80cm (31½in) square thin batting
- 80cm (31½in) square backing fabric
- 5cm (2in) wide fabric scrap strips for binding
- Assorted embroidery threads (stranded and Coton Perlé)
- White or cream quilting thread
- Lightweight cardboard for templates
- Rotary cutter, ruler, mat and pencil
- Sewing machine and general sewing supplies

NOTE: All fabrics are 100 per cent cotton, pre-washed and ironed. A 6mm (¼in) seam allowance is used throughout and is included in the cutting instructions.

Diagram 1
This fence border is pieced using A Blocks for the pickets and B Blocks for the fence rung.

Blocks alternating with seven B Blocks. Add the top and bottom fence borders. From the white print background fabric cut four 4½in squares and join one to each end of the remaining two fence borders. Join the side fence borders with the corner squares attached, taking care to match the corners.

Square up the quilt and sew a 1¼in strip of green background fabric to all four sides.

Using the designs, cut templates and appliqué the three butterflies into position on the corner squares. Appliqué Sunbonnet Sue's watering can.

The Blanket Stitch outline and the back stitch detail on the butterflies are both worked in two strands of embroidery thread. The handles on the watering can are worked in back stitch in two dark green threads.

wide and the third strip 1½in wide. From the white fabric for the runs, cut two strips 1in wide across the width. Join a 2in green strip to a 1in white strip. Add to this a 1in green strip, a 1in white strip and finally, a 1½in green strip (see the diagram below). Cross-cut the pieced strip into 2in wide B Blocks.

For each of the four sides join six A

QUILTING

Sandwich the backing, batting and quilt top and baste firmly. Our Sunbonnet Sue has been quilted by hand. The appliqué designs are outline-quilted working a 1in grid on the diagonal on the background panel behind Sunbonnet Sue. The picket fence, butterflies and watering-can are also outline-quilted.

Green 1½in

White 1in

Green 1in

White 1in

Green 2in

Joining the B Blocks.

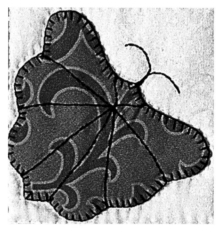

FINISHING

❖

BINDING

Join 2in wide strips of a variety of fabric scraps together to make up four strips each 28in in length.

Before you attach the binding, trim the quilt after quilting to ensure that the edges are square and straight.

Fold the binding strips in half lengthwise with wrong sides together and press with a hot iron. Place the raw edges of the quilt and binding together and attach the side bindings, then the top and bottom bindings.

Turn the bindings over to the back, trimming and folding in the corners and slip stitch them in place.

Sign and date your quilt.

Note: End blocks are smaller

Centre

150%, then 132%

Naive Cushion

*Gather an armful of pretty scraps and create this delightful
basket of flowers on a cushion for your home. This naive cushion uses
traditional appliqué techniques and prairie points
to bring a floral arrangement to life.*

PREPARATION

Trace all shapes onto the cardboard, with the exception of the bias stems, the gingham for the inside of the basket and the three straight strips across the basket.

CUTTING

Cut out the fabric shapes using ¼in seam allowance. In this quilt there are two dark purple leaves, two pink floral leaves, eight light green leaves, six dark green leaves, two floral 'odd' prints, five yellow print leaves and two pink circles. The outer layer of the flower is dark pink and the inner layer is yellow.

Prepare the background by cutting a 16½in square.

CONSTRUCTION

ASSEMBLY

Basket

(Refer to the sewing order diagram.)
Baste the gingham piece (1) to the background, approximately 2½in from the bottom. Appliqué two straight pieces of fabric (2 and 3) to finish a scant ⅜in across the gingham.

Baste, but do not appliqué the strip (4) across the raw edge of the gingham. The top piece (4) finishes approximately ½in wide. Appliqué the basket piece (5) into position.

Stems

Position the bias strips (6, 7 and 8). Turn the raw edges in a scant ¼in on both sides of the strips. Baste the stems to the background. As soon as the stems are in place, finish appliquéing the top of the basket (4).

Leaves

Baste pieces 9 to 29 in position, with the ends under the stems. Appliqué the stems, making sure the inner edge of each curve is appliquéd first.

Small flowers

Appliqué two circles (30 and 31) to cover the raw edges of the stems and flowers. To cover a circle, cut the circle from the cardboard. Cut a piece of fabric twice the size of the cardboard. Sew a running stitch about ⅓in from the raw edge. Place the template on the fabric and pull the thread to gather it tightly. Press the small flowers and remove the template.

Top flower

Place pieces A to F in position. Appliqué them, ensuring that some stitches in F go right through to the background fabric. Threads should not be exposed in the indentations of the flower shapes.

Prairie points

Fold forty 3in squares as shown in Diagram 1. There are ten points for each side of the cushion. Press well. Cut four strips of paper approx 16in x 2in wide. Pin ten of the squares onto each piece of paper, starting and finishing ¼in from each end. Machine through the fabric and the paper ¼in from the lower raw edge.

FINISHED SIZE

- 39cm (15¼in) square

MATERIALS

- 40cm (½yd) of background fabric
- Cushion back: Two rectangles of fabric, each 30cm x 40cm (12in x 16in)
- Prairie point edging: Forty squares of assorted fabric, each 7.5cm (3in)
- Stems: Two bias strips, each 28cm x 2cm (11in x ¾in) and one bias strip 18cm x 2cm (7in x ¾in)
- Basket: 14cm x 7.5cm (5½in x 3in) bias piece of gingham
- 25cm x 20cm (10in x 8in) piece of fabric for the outer edge and three basket strips
- Assorted scraps for leaves and central flower
- 40cm (16in) cushion insert
- Cotton thread to match
- Size 12 appliqué needles
- Two buttons
- Lightweight cardboard
- Tracing paper

Diagram 1
Fold squares as shown for prairie points.

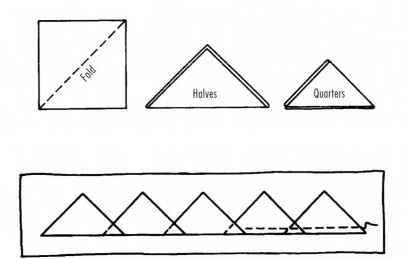

Diagram 2
Pin prairie points to paper and sew ¼in from the lower edge.

Tear the paper away (see Diagram 2).

With the right sides together, sew the triangles to the cushion front, using the machine line from the prairie points as a guide. The points should face inwards (see Diagram 3).

FINISHING

BACKING

Machine a 1in wide hem on the long sides of each backing piece. Work two rows of stitching to add a visual effect. Overlap the two pieces of backing to make a 16in square (see Diagram 4).

With the right sides of the cushion front and the cushion back facing, machine right around all sides, using the machine line from the prairie points as a guide.

Turn the cushion to the right side and finish with two handmade buttonholes and two buttons (see Diagram 5).

Diagram 3
Sew triangles to cushion front with points facing inwards.

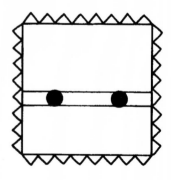

Diagram 5
Make two buttonholes and sew buttons to cushion back.

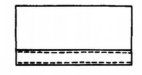 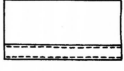 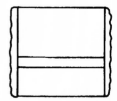

Diagram 4
Sew a 1in hem on the long sides of each backing piece and overlap to make a square.

Numbers denote order of sewing.

*4, *7 and *8   Tack but do not appliqué until stems are in position.

163%

Naive Pine Trees

*Snuggle up under this lovely quilt which features warm-coloured
pine trees on a snow-like background fabric.
It's so easy to make on the sewing machine, you may want to
make more than one in different colour tones.*

PREPARATION

CUTTING

From eleven of the tree fabrics cut two 2in strips, selvedge to selvedge. From the twelfth fabric cut three 2in strips selvedge to selvedge. (A total of twenty-five strips). Using templates 2 to 6, from these strips, cut two trees from each of the first eleven colours and three trees from the twelfth colour. Note that the template for tree pieces 3 and 6 is the same.

From the tree trunk fabric cut two 2in strips from selvedge to selvedge and from these cut twenty-five tree trunks using template 7.

From the main background fabric cut twenty-five 2in strips, selvedge to selvedge – each strip is enough for one block. Cut the background pieces with the strips folded selvedge to selvedge – this will automatically give you the reverse (R) pieces. Template 1 is the reverse of template 8 – one of each is required for each block.

CONSTRUCTION

Join the background pieces to the corresponding tree pieces in strips (see Diagram 1). A quick method is to join all the background pieces to the right-hand side of the tree pieces in chain fashion, cut the threads, then join all the left-hand side background pieces.

Join the eight rows of the block together.

Before going any further, it is important to trim all the tree blocks to an 8½in square. When trimming, use a centre line to make sure the tree sits in the centre of each block.

FINISHED SIZE

- 140cm (55in) square
- Block size 21.5cm (8½in)

MATERIALS

- 2.3m (2½yd) main light background fabric
- 90cm (1yd) contrasting light background fabric for sashing
- 20cm (¼yd) each of twelve different prints for trees
- 60cm (⅔yd) of dark print for tree trunks and binding
- 3m (3⅓yd) Pellon or batting
- 2.3m (2½yd) fabric for backing
- Template plastic
- Rotary cutter, ruler and cutting mat
- Sewing machine
- Quilting thread

NOTE: The templates are provided on the Pattern Sheet and include a 6mm (¼in) seam allowance. The arrow on the templates and instructions indicates the straight of the grain. Accurate piecing is important in the construction of this quilt.

Diagram 1
Block layout diagram.
B = background
R = reverse
TT = tree trunk

*Piece the block
together in rows.*

Diagram 2
Cut and piece the backing fabric.

Diagram 3
Quilting design.

From the main background fabric cut twelve half squares and four corners using the templates provided. From the contrast background fabric cut fourteen 2in strips for the sashings.

Decide on the placement of the trees, then join them in rows diagonally, adding sashings between each block and a half square (or quarter square on the corners) to each end (see colour photograph).

Starting from the bottom left, join the rows, adding top and bottom sashings to each row. Sew the long sashings, then join the centre four sashings.

ASSEMBLY

❖

Remove the selvedges from the backing fabric. Cut and join it as shown in Diagram 2. Sandwich the backing, batting and quilt top and baste or pin them together ready for quilting.

Each block in this quilt has been quilted all over, regardless of the trees, with straight lines of parallel quilting a half inch apart, alternating blocks of diagonal, horizontal and vertical lines (see Diagram 3).

FINISHING

❖

BINDING

From the binding fabric cut 3in strips. Join them into a piece long enough to go around the quilt. Press the binding in half lengthwise – raw edges together. Stitch it to the front through all thicknesses, leaving a flap for finishing and mitring the corners. Turn to the back and firmly slip stitch in place. Sign and date your quilt.

Cottage Gardens Wall-hanging

*Quaint naive-style cottages are joined together
with colourful floral fabrics to make this whimsical
country village wall-hanging which is decorated
with easy appliqué and Broderie Perse flowers.*

PREPARATION

FABRICS

Each block in this quilt is framed by a white border so that it stands alone. The overall colour coordination is therefore not a problem.

Choose colours from the flower fabric for each block. Most of the fabrics contain green leaves which will assist with the choice of grass colours: blue, blue-green, green or yellow-green. Choose the various blues for the sky. The houses are best worked in dark colours, with a light window, door and chimney.

CUTTING

Each block is made up of five strips. Four are 2in wide and the strip representing the grass at the bottom is 2½in wide. Working up from the widest strip and referring to the rows in the diagram, cut the following:

From the medium green fabric (Row 5), cut sixteen pieces 2½in x 8½in or four strips across the fabric 2½in wide. Cut these pieces into 8½in lengths.

From the light green fabric (Row 4, to go next to medium green), cut sixteen pieces 2in x 8½in or four strips across the fabric 2in wide. Cut these pieces into 8½in lengths.

From the very light green fabric (Row 3, to go next to light green), cut sixteen pieces 2in x 8½in or four strips across the fabric 2in wide. Cut these pieces into 8½in lengths.

From the very light blue fabric (Row 2, to go next to very light green), cut sixteen pieces 2in x 8½in or four strips across the fabric 2in wide. Cut these pieces into 8½in lengths.

From the light blue fabric (Row 1, to go next to very light blue), cut sixteen pieces 2in x 8½in or four strips across the fabric 2in wide. Cut these pieces into 8½in lengths.

FINISHED SIZE

- 112cm (44in square)
- Block size 21.5cm (8½in)

MATERIALS

- **Garden flowers:** Medium-scale florals with clearly defined flower edges

- **Cottages:** Dark coloured scraps for roofs and walls; yellow-toned fabrics for the chimney, door and window

- **Grass:** Green small scale prints, shading from very light, light and medium green

- **Strips for the grass:** 30cm (⅓yd) medium green fabric, 25cm (⅓yd) light green fabric, 25cm (⅓yd) very light green fabric

- **Sky:** Small-scale blue prints, shading from very pale blue to pale blue, 25cm (⅓yd) pale blue fabric, 25cm (⅓yd) very pale blue fabric

- **Frames:** 45cm (½yd) white fabric

- **Sashing:** 70cm (¾yd) medium-scale floral fabric, or forty pieces of floral fabric ranging from light to dark, each 23cm x 6.5cm (9in x 2½in)

- **Setting squares:** 20cm (¼yd) small-scale floral print, or twenty-five 6.5cm (2½in) squares ranging from dark to light

- 1.3m (1½yd) fabric for backing and hanging sleeve

- 20cm (¼yd) small-scale floral fabric with black background for the binding

- 115cm (45in) square of batting

- Vliesofix or iron-on appliqué paper

- Pencil

- Scissors

- Black cotton thread for appliqué

- Beige thread for piecing

- Quilting thread

- Sewing machine

- Rotary cutter, ruler and cutting mat

NOTE: All strips cut for the piece blocks include 6mm (¼in) seams.

Pieced block with cottage and flowers appliquéd in Blanket Stitch.

CONSTRUCTION

In this quilt, the palest colours in each block are situated at the top. Each block is made up of five 8½in wide strips. Working from the top, arrange the 2in x 8½in strips in the following sequence: Row 1 (blue), Row 2 (pale blue), Row 3 (very light green) and Row 4 (light green). Row 5 (medium green) is 2½in x 8½in. Sew the strips in sequence. Press all the seams down using a hot iron.

Make sixteen blocks.

Row 1	2in
Row 2	2in
Row 3	2in
Row 4	2in
Row 5	2½in

Diagram for grading background colours for each block.

APPLIQUE

Following the pattern, trace the separate parts of the cottages onto the paper side of the Vliesofix.

Cut out the shapes roughly. Press them onto the wrong side of the selected fabrics. Cut out the shapes along the lines, peel off the paper and position them onto the background. Select your choice of flowers and back each one with the Vliesofix.

Position the flowers around the house in a pleasing arrangement and iron them in place.

Work a small Blanket Stitch around all the raw edges of the flowers, using the black cotton thread.

For the frames, cut the white fabric into fifteen ¾in wide strips. For each block, cross-cut into two 8½in strips for the sides and two 9½in strips for the top and bottom. Attach these to the sides first, then to the top and bottom. Press the seams towards the block.

For the sashings, use the medium-scale florals. Cut the fabric into 9in x 2½in strips. If you are using only one fabric, cut this into 2½in wide strips across the fabric, then cross-cut these strips into 9in long pieces.

For the setting squares, use a range of small-scale floral prints to cut twenty-five 2½in squares ranging from dark to light, or cut the squares from one fabric only.

NOTE: Study the photograph and note that the sashing is graded from light to dark while the setting squares are from dark to light, working from the top left-hand corner of the quilt.

Lay out the completed squares with the sashing strips and the setting squares. Sew them together in rows, then join the rows, taking care to match the joins

ASSEMBLY

Cut a 4in strip from the backing fabric and set it aside to make up the hanging sleeve. Cut the remaining backing fabric into a 44in square. Sandwich the completed top together with the batting and backing. Baste or pin the layers together.

Hand quilt or machine quilt depending on your preference.

The Cottage Gardens quilt featured has been quilted both sides of the white frames and right around each of the setting squares.

FINISHING

BINDING

Cut the binding fabric into five 1½in strips. With wrong sides together, attach these strips to the top and bottom of the quilt. Attach the binding strips to the sides, neatening the corners as you sew. Turn the binding neatly over to the back of the quilt and slip stitch it down by hand.

Make a hanging sleeve. Attach it to the back of the quilt and insert a rod.

Don't forget to sign and date your quilt, then sit back and enjoy.

COTTAGE TEMPLATES

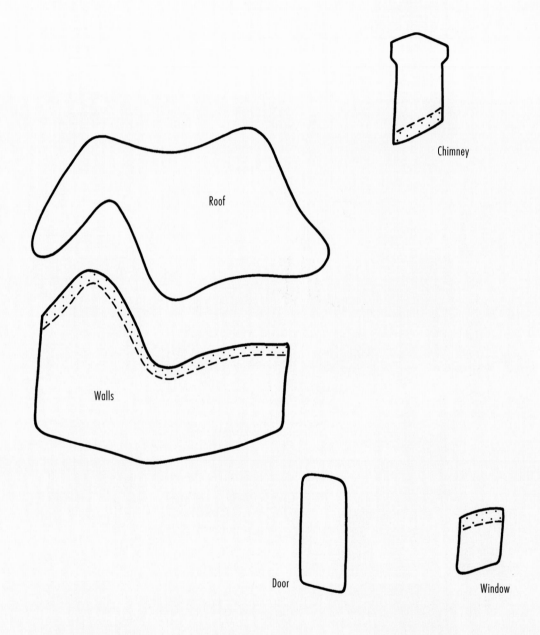

Chimney

Roof

Walls

Door

Window

Appletree Grove

*Tiny print fabrics and antiqued colours combine to make
a miniature quilt full of country charm. Combining appliqué piecing,
embroidery and quilting, this little quilt is a fine example
of what can be achieved on a small scale.*

FINISHED SIZE

- 11½in x 14in (29cm x 36cm)

MATERIALS

- **The background:** 15cm x 55cm (6in x 22in) each of four light fabrics
- **Stars, outer border and binding:** 25cm (⅓yd) dark red fabric
- **Apples:** 15cm (6in) square bright red fabric
- **First tree and apple leaves:** 15cm (6in) square green fabric
- **Second tree:** 10cm (4in) square green fabric
- **Sign and tree trunks:** 15cm (6in) square wood grain brown fabric
- **Hearts and checkerboard:** 15cm x 55cm (6in x 22in) each of two blues
- **Inside border:** 15cm x 55cm (6in x 22in) plain dark blue
- 40cm x 50cm (16in x 20in) thin batting
- 40cm x 50cm (16in x 20in) backing fabric
- 5 red buttons
- Embroidery thread (dark brown, red and green)
- Sewing threads and quilting thread to match fabrics
- Needle to appliqué
- Freezer paper
- HB pencil and scissors
- Sewing machine

NOTE: 6mm (¼in) seam allowance is included in all cutting instructions.

A dashed line on an appliqué template pattern indicates that the seam does not need to be basted under.

PREPARATION

❖

CUTTING

Cut fabric pieces to the following sizes.

Red stars: 5in x 2¾in
Green sign: 4in x 4¼in
Beige trees: 5in x 4½in
Two blue hearts: 4in x 3in
Green apples: 8½in x 3in
Two blue checked strips: 1in x 22in; 2 background colours – 1in x 22in
Plain blue inside border: two strips 1in x 11¼in; two strips 1in x 9½in
Red outside border: two strips 2in x 12¼in and two strips 2in x 13in
Red binding: two strips 2in x 44in

From the freezer paper trace and cut two stars, two hearts, four apples, four leaves, trees, sign and signpost.

CONSTRUCTION

❖

APPLIQUE

Following the instructions for the freezer paper appliqué technique, prepare and sew all pieces to the background pieces.

Freezer paper method
Place the freezer paper shiny side down on the appliqué pattern and trace the design using an HB pencil. Carefully cut out the freezer paper shapes. Do not add seam allowances.

Place the shiny side of the freezer paper template on the wrong side of the fabric. Using a medium to hot iron, press the freezer paper template to the fabric. One reasonably quick press should be sufficient. Cut out the fabric around the freezer paper, adding ¼in seam allowance.

Step 1
Cut out template shapes from freezer paper and iron onto the fabrics.

Working with the right side of the appliqué towards you, fold the seam allowance over the freezer paper and baste, stitching through all layers. Turn over a little at a time and use small, even tacking stitches.

HELPFUL HINT

When the shape is completely tacked, trim the seam allowance back to a generous ⅛in.

Pin the shape to the background and appliqué in place using blind hemming stitch. Keep these stitches small and even, placing approximately two stitches to every ⅛in. Remove the basting stitches.

If there is an opening somewhere in the appliqué (for example, the first tree and the upright signpost), remove the freezer paper using a small pair of tweezers. If there is no opening and the appliqué has been completely stitched, turn the section over and make a small slit in the background fabric, behind the appliqué and gently remove the freezer paper through this opening. Press the completed appliqué on the wrong side using a medium to hot steam iron.

EMBROIDERY

Using the dark brown embroidery thread, Chain Stitch the 'hangers' from the sign to the signpost. With an HB pencil, lightly print the word 'APPLES' on the sign, then embroider with the red thread using a back stitch. Use the green thread to make various-sized straight stitches to represent the grass.

Checkerboard
Sew one blue strip and one strip of the background fabric together. Press the

Step 2
Leave a small opening when appliquéing so that the freezer paper can be removed.

seam towards the blue. Cut into 1in sections. Sew these sections to form eight pairs, making sure you reverse the top section to form the checkerboard pattern. Press the seams open. Sew the larger sections together to form the complete checkerboard section. Make a second checkerboard with the two remaining strips.

ASSEMBLY

Set out all the completed sections and sew them together in the following order. Sew the stars to the trees, then the signpost to the hearts. Sew these two sections together and add the apple section. Sew one checkerboard to the top and one to the bottom. Press these seams away from the checkerboard.

Sew the narrow inner borders to the sides of the completed centre section and press the seams outwards. Finish by adding the top and bottom inner borders. You may like to trim ⅛in off this border to give a good straight edge, ready for the next border.

Sew the outer border on in the same order as the inner border. Press all seams outwards. This border can be trimmed if you prefer a narrower width.

QUILTING

Sandwich the quilt top, batting and backing. Baste or pin the layers together.

Quilt first around all the appliqué motifs, then around the inner and outer borders. Cross-hatch all over, stopping only when an appliqué motif is reached and continuing on the other side of the motif. Mark the cross-hatching lines using quilter's tape.

FINISHING

BINDING

Before adding the binding, trim off the excess batting and backing from the quilt. Join the two binding strips together and press in half along the length of the strip. Leaving a 2in tail, commence sewing halfway along one side, the raw edges of the binding aligning with the raw edges on the right side of the quilt. Stop sewing ¼in from the end of this side. Mitre the corner by folding the binding up to make a right angle, then fold the binding down the next side. The folded binding will be level with all the raw edges.

Continue to sew and mitre each corner of the quilt. When you have sewn right around the quilt, return to the starting point and pin and join the ends carefully. Trim any excess binding. Turn the binding to the back of the quilt and slip stitch it down by hand.

Sew five red buttons onto the apple trees as in the photograph.

It is important that you document all information about your quilt onto a piece of fabric, using either a permanent marker pen or a needle and thread. Slip stitch the fabric to the back of the quilt. Sign and date your quilt and add any other interesting information. Generations to come will thank you for it.

When enlarged height should measure 10½in.

When enlarged width should measure 8¼in.

133%

Shenandoah Floral Appliqué

The graceful design and fresh colours in this appealing quilt
make it worthy of the time needed to stitch it.
Swirling daffodil blocks are enhanced by the swag border
and all appliqué shapes are outlined in black with fine Blanket Stitch.

PREPARATION

❖

TEMPLATES

Draft and cut a 16in square and an 11in square from white cardboard. Refer to the Pattern Sheet for the block diagram, borders and corner templates. Make a full-size 16in copy of the daffodil block on page 121, which shows one-quarter of the design. Trace off templates for all pieces onto cardboard, showing grainlines and the identifying letter, then cut apart. Trace and make templates for the corner swag unit, the swags for the sides and top, leaves and buds. The side swag is larger than the top swag, but the leaves and the buds are the same. Show the grainlines on all templates.

CUTTING

Background

Prepare fifteen squares for the background by tracing around the 16in template on the wrong side of the fabric. Leave ½in seam allowance all around and cut out the squares. This is to allow for possible shrinkage of the block during stitching. The block will be squared off to 16½in before being pieced with the other blocks.

Corners

Cut four squares with the 11in template by tracing on the wrong side of the fabric and leave ¼in seam allowance all around.

Borders

On the lengthwise grain, cut two 11½in x 82in pieces for the side borders, and two 11½in x 50in pieces for the top and bottom borders. These will be adjusted to the correct size before attaching them to the assembled blocks.

Use a scant ¼in seam allowance around all templates. For each block, cut the required number of pieces according to the numbers on the pattern.

A, B and C are bias strips. Cut strips for A, ⅞in wide and for B and C, ¾in wide. Templates D to M are traced on the wrong side of the fabric and cut out with a seam allowance. It may be useful to iron the fabric with spray starch to make the edges crisp.

CONSTRUCTION

BLOCKS

For each block, lay a background square right side up, centred over the block drawing and tape into position. Lightly trace the design onto the fabric with a pencil or water-soluble pen, drawing inside the lines. This will help in positioning the pieces onto the background.

For the bias strips, cut into the lengths required by the templates and include a seam allowance at both ends. Press in both bias edges to the wrong side to make strips approximately ⅜in wide for A and ¼in wide for B and C. It is not necessary to iron in the raw edges of each end of the stems, the bottom of the buds or where a piece will be overlapped by another, such as the tops of the swags or the sides of the leaves.

FINISHED SIZE

- approx. 179cm x 260cm (70½in x 102½in)
- Block size 40cm (16in) square

MATERIALS

- 6.2m (6¾yd) white or off-white fabric
- 1.2m (1⅓yd) plain green fabric
- 1.2m (1⅓yd) plain yellow fabric for swags and trumpet of daffodils
- 1.3m (1½yd) lighter yellow fabric for daffodils and binding
- 30cm (⅓yd) plain orange fabric for buds
- 5.7m (6¼yd) white backing fabric
- Queen-size batting, low loft
- Cotton thread to match appliqué colours
- 2 rolls black cotton thread
- Quilting thread
- 2 sheets white poster cardboard for templates
- Mechanical pencil with 0.5mm lead, HB or 2B
- Water-soluble marking pen
- Spray starch (optional)
- General sewing supplies, including No 11 Sharps for appliqué and No 9 crewel needles

NOTE: It is suggested that fabrics be 100 per cent cotton, pre-washed and ironed. Fabric requirements are based on 108cm (42½in) wide fabric.

Instructions are given for hand appliqué. Assemble blocks and borders with 6mm (¼in) seam allowance throughout. This method of appliqué is used because the pieces are attached with Blanket Stitch. If you prefer to use only blind stitch, then use the appliqué method of your choice.

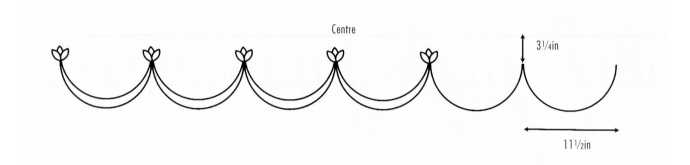

Centre

3¼in

11½in

Diagram 1
Position of side swags. Attach the swags,
then buds and leaves.

Prepare the other appliqué pieces by placing the appropriate template on the wrong side of the fabric, pin into the ironing board and press in the seam allowance over the template. Clip where necessary, fold points neatly and aim for smooth edges. Use the tip of the iron and avoid burning your fingers. Remove the template each time.

Pieces are attached in alphabetical order commencing with bias stem A. Refer to the block layout. Pin each piece in position one at a time and attach with blind stitch, using thread to match the appliqué piece. Make fifteen blocks.

Outline all the pieces with Blanket Stitch on the edge. Use a double thread of black and make these stitches no more than ⅛in apart.

Before pressing the blocks, sponge off all water-soluble pen markings if used. Press the blocks on the wrong side, face down on a towel. Square up each block, if necessary, with the master template.

BORDERS

Using the templates shown on the Pattern Sheet, cut out and prepare all the swag pieces, buds and leaves as described.

To make the corners for each block, crease the square on a diagonal. Place the bottom tip of the prepared swag, centred on the diagonal, 3¼in from the corner marked on the back of the block. Pin or baste into position and attach with a blind stitch. Attach the buds and leaves.

For the side borders, there are six swags along each side. Fold each length

in half and crease. Starting from the centre, mark the position of each swag with a pencil, 11½in apart and 3¼in down from the top raw edge (see Diagram 1). Lightly mark the bottom curve of the swag as a placement guide if you wish. Attach the swags, then buds, then leaves.

To make the top and bottom borders, there are four swags along each border, slightly smaller than the side swags and placed closer together. Fold the length in half, crease and start from the centre to mark the position of each swag with a pencil. Swags are 11in apart and 3¼in down from the top raw edge. Attach as for the sides.

Blanket Stitch around each piece as for the daffodil blocks. Press as above.

ASSEMBLY

Join three blocks together into a row and make five rows. Press the seams in the opposite directions in alternate rows. Join rows to make the central section of the quilt top and press.

Measure through the centre, width-wise and lengthwise and note the measurements. Adjust the length of the side and the top and bottom borders to correspond, ensuring that you make equal adjustments from each end.

Sew on the side borders, matching the centre points with the quilt top. Sew a corner block to each end of the

QUILTING

The design in each block is outline-quilted, as are the swags. A simple curved design forms a lattice between the blocks, with a flower at each junction. Cross-hatch the quilt 1½in apart to fill in the background area and borders, using a white quilting thread. Alternatively, use quilting patterns of your choice and mark these on the top of the quilt before basting. Layer the quilt top, batting and backing, pin together randomly and baste in a grid of 5in to 6in squares. Quilt as desired.

FINISHING

BINDING

Remove the basting and trim batting and backing level with the quilt top. The light yellow fabric is used to make a double-fold bias binding 3⅜in wide. A 32in square is needed for the continuous bias method and bias strips are cut 2½in wide to yield approximately 11yd of binding. Press the binding in half length-wise, then pin to the quilt top, mitring the corners. Sew with a ⅜in seam, fold the binding to the back of the quilt and slip stitch it neatly in place.

Sign your name and date on the quilt with either a label, embroidery stitching or a fine permanent marking pen.

top and bottom borders. Sew the two side borders to the top and bottom. Using a hot iron, press across the entire quilt top.

BACKING

Cut the backing fabric in half across the width, remove the selvedges and sew two long sides together. Press the seam open. Trim the backing to 3in larger than the quilt top on all sides. Cut the batting to the same size as the backing.

QUARTER BLOCK DESIGN

Numbers indicate number of pieces for one block.

Appliqué pieces are in alphabetical order.

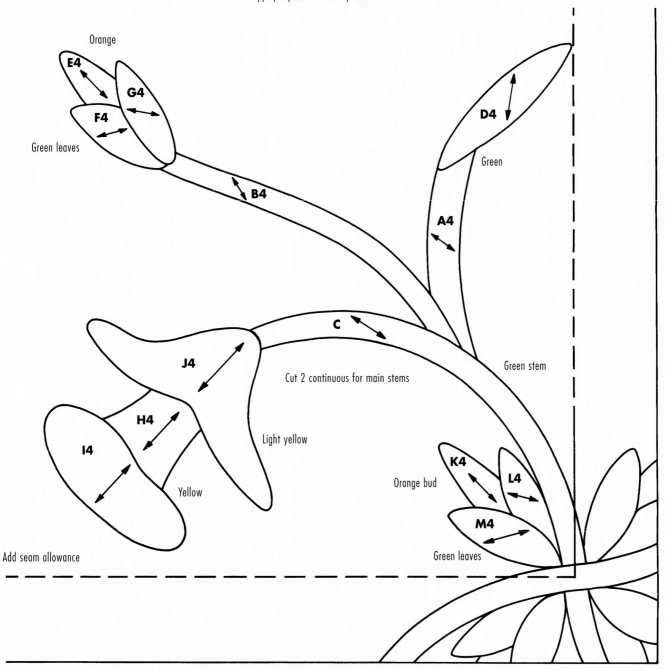

Orange

E4

G4

F4

Green leaves

B4

D4

Green

A4

C

J4

Green stem

Cut 2 continuous for main stems

H4

Light yellow

I4

Yellow

K4

Orange bud

L4

M4

Add seam allowance

Green leaves

112%

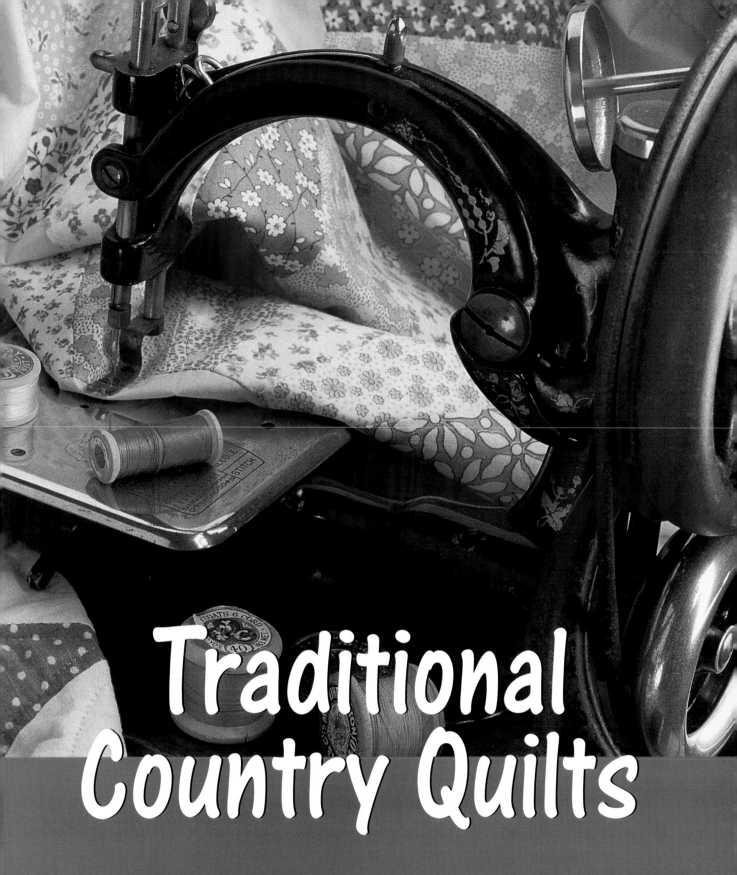

Traditional Country Quilts

For many centuries, in every household, rich or poor, women have sewn.
Patchwork quilts are characteristic of country life. Originally, these quilts
were made from small pieces of fabric left over from old clothing.
Today, choosing fabrics for country quilts is made very easy
with entire ranges devoted to the theme.

Rustic Pinwheel Quilt

*Made from scrap fabrics in mellow tones, this wondrous quilt
which is perfect as a queen-size throw or a double bed quilt,
evokes country days of old. The traditional Pinwheel Block is arranged
in a pattern that is quick and simple to sew.*

PREPARATION

CUTTING

From each of the twenty dark fabrics, cut nine 4½in squares, then cut them in half on the diagonal. From each of the twenty light to medium fabrics, cut nine 4½in squares and cut them in half on the diagonal. This will give you three hundred and sixty dark and three hundred and sixty medium to light triangles.

CONSTRUCTION

PINWHEEL BLOCK

Match the light triangles to the dark triangles in random pairs. With wrong sides together and sewing on the long edge of the triangle, chain-piece all the triangles together, using a ¼in seam allowance (see diagram). If you wish to copy this design, ensure that the four light triangles in each square are the same print.

Clip the threads, separate the pieces and press the seams towards the dark fabric. It is important, at this stage, to stack the squares in two piles.

Match the light to the dark fabric and sew the two squares together to form a half-block (see photograph). For speed of assembly, these half-blocks can also be chain-pieced at this time.

Press the seams towards the dark fabric and divide them into two piles. Keeping the light to dark sequence for the sections, match two half-blocks, taking care to match the centre points by pinning them together. Sew the two half blocks together to complete the block. You will need a total of ninety blocks.

FINISHED SIZE

- approximately 225cm x 206cm (89in x 81in)
- Block size 18cm (7in)

MATERIALS

- 20cm (¼yd) each of twenty different dark fabrics (or a total of 2.5m (2¾yd) of dark fabrics or an assortment of dark scraps to cut one hundred and eighty 11.5cm (4½in) squares)
- 20cm (¼yd) each of twenty different light/medium fabrics (or a total of 2.5m (2¾yd) light/medium fabrics or an assortment of light/medium scraps to cut one hundred and eighty 11.5cm (4½in) squares)
- 2.25m (2½yd) contrast fabric for sashing and border
- 5m (5½yd) fabric for backing
- 235cm x 220cm (94in x 86in) of queen-size batting
- 70cm (¾yd) fabric for binding
- Rotary cutter, mat and ruler
- Sewing machine and dark beige thread

Join pairs of block sections alternating light and dark triangles.

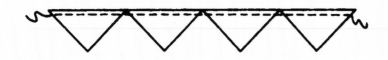

Chain-piecing the triangles.

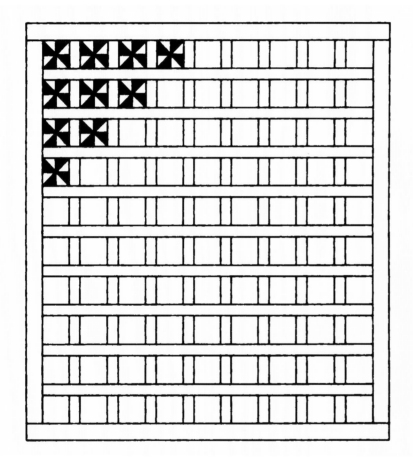

Quilt layout diagram.

eight blocks. Sew the eight blocks together and add an extra block to the end of each row (see quilt layout diagram). Make ten rows.

Press seams towards the sashing. Sew a 2¼yd long sashing strip to each row of blocks. Pin rows together in pairs, taking care to align the short sashing strips. Sew the pairs of rows together. Trim off the excess and press the seams towards the sashing.

Sew the 3in border fabric to the sides first, then to the top and bottom, trimming the length to fit.

Fold the backing fabric and cut it in half from selvedge to selvedge. Cut off the selvedge, place right sides together and join the two halves. Sandwich the backing, batting and top together and pin or baste into place. Cross-hatch the quilt through the centre of each block and on either side of the sashing strips. The geometric pattern is also suitable if you wish to tie the quilt.

FINISHING

BINDING

Trim away any excess backing and batting from the edges.

Cut the binding fabric into 3in wide strips, selvedge to selvedge.

Sew the strips together to form one long strip, fold the strips in half with the wrong sides together and press along the length of the strip.

Starting at the centre bottom of the quilt, sew the binding to the quilt top with all raw edges together, ½in from the edge. Mitre the corners as you go and overlap the ends to finish.

Fold the binding to the back of the quilt and slip stitch it in place with a matching thread.

Make a label for the back of the quilt and sign and date it.

ASSEMBLY

Cut four 3in wide strips by the length of the sashing fabric which is 2½yd and reserve this for the outside border.

Cut the remainder of the sashing fabric into 2in strips. Reserve nine 2¼yd long strips for the cross-sashing and cross-cut the remainder of the sashing into eighty 7½in sections.

The quilt is made up of ten rows of nine blocks. For each row, sew a 7½in sashing strip to the right side of each

Rainy's Quilt

*This delightful country-style blue scrap quilt featuring
the Remembrance block was machine pieced
and hand quilted. As an interesting touch,
the blocks have been taken across into the border.*

PREPARATION

CUTTING

When you are cutting the fabric requirements for a quilt, it is always advisable to cut the larger pieces first and the smallest pieces last.

Outer borders

From the assortment of light blue and beige fabrics, cut eighteen rectangles, 2in x 11in. For each rectangle, measure from the corner in 1¼in along the long side and mark it at this point, then measure 1¼in along the short side and mark it.

Align the ruler to these two points and carefully trim off the triangles. Repeat at the other end of the rectangle. These pieces are for the sides of the outer border (see Diagram 1).

From the same assortment of fabric prints, cut eight rectangles measuring 2in x 7¾in to make up the corner sections. Place four pieces of fabric right side up and four pieces of fabric right side down. On one end of the rectangle, measure and mark 1¼in as shown previously and carefully trim off the triangle. At the opposite end of the rectangle measure across 2in and mark it. Align the ruler carefully to the 2in mark and the top corner of the rectangle and cut off this corner at this point.

Edge triangles

From the dark blue fabrics, cut nine 6⅞in squares. Cut each square across the diagonal to produce a total of eighteen triangles for the outer edge. Cut two 5⅛in squares, then cut across the diagonal. These make up the four corner triangles.

Lattices

From the light fabrics, cut one hundred and twenty 6½in x 2in rectangles to be used for the lattices.

From the dark fabrics, cut seventy-one squares, each 2in. These are the intersection squares for the lattices.

BINDING

From the navy fabric, cut seven 2¼in strips wide across the width of the fabric for the binding.

BLOCKS

Using mainly medium and dark fabrics, cut one hundred 3⅞in squares. Cut each square across the diagonal. Each block requires four of these triangles of the same fabric, so cut two squares from each fabric. Set these triangles aside in a pile, these are the outer B triangles (see Diagram 2).

Using mainly light and medium fabrics, cut twenty-five 3⅞in squares, then cut each across the diagonal. These will form the central B triangles. Only one

FINISHED SIZE

- 144cm x 170cm (56¾in x 67in)
- Block size 15cm (6in)

MATERIALS

- 20cm (¼yd) each of twenty-five assorted prints
- 50cm (⅔yd) plain navy fabric for binding
- 3.3m (3¾yd) backing fabric
- 170cm x 190cm (67in x 75in) batting
- Rotary cutter, board, ruler
- Quilter's pencil
- Quilting thread
- Neutral sewing thread (mid-grey)

NOTE: It is suggested that fabrics be 100 per cent cotton, 112cm (45in) wide, pre-washed and ironed.

Check your scrap stash before purchasing your fabrics. Scrap quilts are enhanced by the use of a maximum of prints. Charm packs are available from most shops and will assist in increasing your variety of prints.

Another wonderful way to bring 'life' to a scrap quilt is to use small amounts of closely related colours. While this is an essentially 'blue' quilt, there are small amounts of green and black fabrics and an occasional scrap of beige fabric.

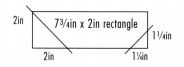

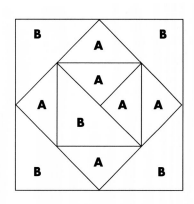

Diagram 1
Border Sections.

Diagram 2
Remembrance Block Construction Diagram.

triangle is required for each block.

From the light, medium and dark fabrics, choose an even mix of colours and prints and cut fifty 4¼in squares. Cut each square across both diagonals, so as to create four triangles. You should now have a total of two hundred of these triangles. These make up the outer round of A triangles and four triangles of the same fabric are required for each block. Set these triangles aside in a separate pile.

Again, from the light, medium and dark fabrics choose a different even mix of fabrics and cut twenty-five 4¼in squares. Cut each square across both diagonals to make a total of one hundred triangles. These triangles form the central A pieces and two different print fabrics are required for each block.

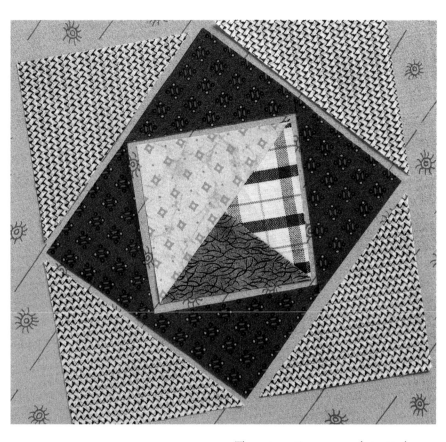

The centre section sewn, ready to attach the A triangles.

CONSTRUCTION

❖

Refer to the block construction diagram and the step-by-step photograph on page 129.

Select two different central A triangles and sew them together, creating a larger triangle. Sew a central B triangle to the pieced triangle from the previous step. Press the seam towards the B triangle. This becomes the central square. Sew an outer A triangle to either side of the central square and press outwards.

Sew remaining two triangles to each of the other sides and press outwards.

Sew a round of outer B triangles, all of the same fabric, to the central piece. Begin with two opposite sides, pressed outwards, then the other two sides, pressed outwards.

Remember to press each seam from the right side as you sew as this ensures flatter, more accurate piecing. Make a total of fifty blocks.

ASSEMBLY

❖

Refer to the quilt assembly diagram and lay out the completed blocks in a diagonal setting. Rearrange the sequence of the blocks if necessary to provide a balanced look. There is no 'right way' to position the blocks so place them randomly as you choose.

Arrange the lattice strips and intersection squares and lastly the outer triangles and border sections.

To make up the rows, sew a border section to the top and left side of the top left corner triangle. Commencing at the inner corner, sew a mitred seam between the two border sections. Press the seams towards the borders.

Pin each section carefully before you begin sewing. Fold the lattice in half and finger-press it together, then pin it down so that it aligns with the seam in the centre of the block.

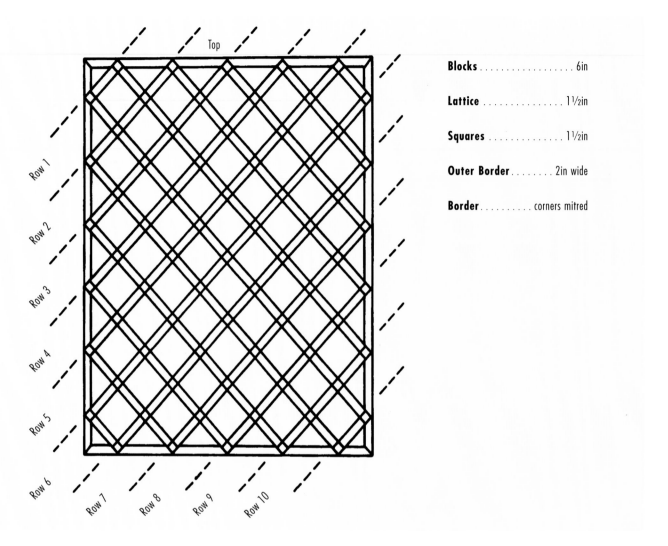

Quilt layout diagram.

Blocks 6in

Lattice 1½in

Squares 1½in

Outer Border . . . . 2in wide

Border . . . . corners mitred

Row 1

Sew the lattice strips to either side of the first block, then press the seams towards the lattices (this is the same throughout the quilt top).

Sew a square to either end of the lattice above the block, press. Sew this unit to the block, press. Sew the large outer triangles to the border sections, press towards the border. Sew these units to either side of the block.

The large triangles have bias edges, so take extra care with the pinning, sewing and pressing. Sew with the bias edge uppermost to prevent excess stretching.

Sew the corner section to the upper edge of Row 1. Sew the set-in seams at either end. Sew these small seams from the squares to the outer edge of the quilt.

Row 2

Sew the four squares and three lattices above the next row of blocks, press. Join the three blocks with the four lattices. Sew these two strips to each other, matching seams carefully, then press.

Sew the border triangles and border sections to each other as previously described and sew these to either end of the row.

Sew row 1 and 2 together, carefully pinning all the intersections. Sew the small set-in seams at either end as before.

Rows 3–5

Sew these rows in the same manner, noting that row 5 has a corner section on the right-hand edge. Set the top half of the quilt aside.

Rows 10–6

Sew rows 10 to 6, beginning with the bottom right corner, then row 10 and working back towards the centre, as described for the other half of the quilt. Make up the row of lattices and squares required for between rows 5 and 6, press. Sew to the lower edge of row 6 and press again. Sew the two halves together and press them well.

BACKING

Fold the 3¾yd backing fabric in half, right sides together, raw edge to raw edge. Using a ½in seam and commencing at the raw edge, sew down to the fold. Trim off the selvedges. Cut open along the fold line, press the seam open.

QUILTING

Press the top and backing well. Lay out the backing with the wrong side up and with the seam running across the quilt. Smooth out the wrinkles. Place the batting on top and smooth it out, then centre the pieced top, right side up.

Baste the quilt in a grid pattern, at approximately 5in intervals.

Roll any excess batting and backing to the front edge of the quilt and baste this securely.

The quilting design is hand-quilted with a 1½in diagonal grid pattern. The border section has three parallel lines that are quilted ⅜in apart.

Once the quilting is complete, remove the basting threads and lay the quilt out on a smooth surface. Carefully trim the edges of the batting and backing to align with the edges of the pieced top. Check that all corners are square, square them off and trim if necessary.

FINISHING

BINDING

Using the seven 2¼in wide strips, sew them together with bias seams. Press the seams open. Fold the strip lengthwise with right sides out. Set the machine to a slighter longer stitch length. Align all of the raw edges and sew with a generous ¼in seam allowance.

Turn the binding to the back of the quilt and hand sew in place.

Sign and date your quilt.

Arkansas Troubles

Colourful scrap fabrics from the 1930s against a background
of white homespun make up this delightful antique quilt.
This traditional quilt uses the Arkansas Troubles Block,
a variation of the Drunkard's Path Block.

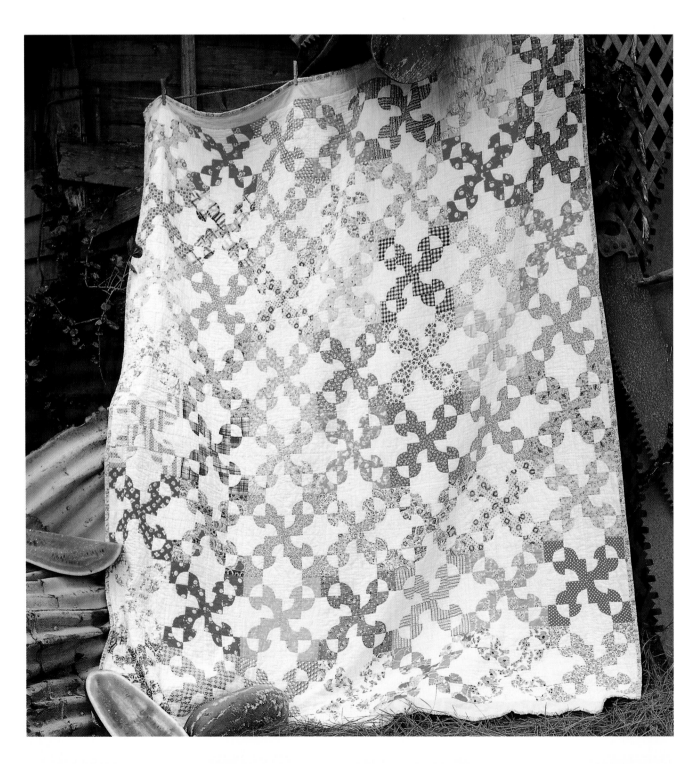

PREPARATION

TEMPLATES

Refer to the diagrams for templates A and B. Trace the outline onto template plastic and mark the grainline and matching points. Templates are the finished size. A ¼in seam allowance must be added when cutting the fabric pieces.

CUTTING

There are fifty-six Arkansas Troubles Blocks. Mark around the templates on the wrong side of the fabric, keeping the grain correct and adding ¼in seam allowances all around. This is where the quilter's wheel can be used with great ease around the curves. Using a propelling pencil, place the tip in the hole in the wheel, then place the edge of the wheel against the edge of the template. Holding the template firmly, move the wheel around the template to mark the

seam allowance (see step-by-step photograph). If you do not have a quilter's wheel handy, use a quilter's ruler to mark the ¼in seam allowance around each of the templates.

Each block requires eight A pieces and eight B pieces from the same print fabric and eight As and eight Bs from the white homespun fabric. Cut a total of fifty-six blocks, using different prints.

CONSTRUCTION

BLOCK
CONSTRUCTION

Refer to the positioning of the completed block in Step 3 on the following page. When you are sewing this block, it will be necessary to pin the curves stretching them to fit as you go.

Join Patterns A and B together using a

FINISHED SIZE

• 178cm x 203cm (70in x 80in)

• Block size 25cm (10in) square

MATERIALS

• 3.8m (4¼yd) white homespun

• 5.6m (6¼yd) assorted prints (scraps or squares at least 30cm (12in) or 10cm (4in) each of fifty-six prints

• 60cm (⅔yd) print fabric for binding

• 4.5m (5yd) backing fabric

• Single-bed size low-loft or cotton batting

• Neutral sewing thread

• Quilting thread

• Template material (preferably plastic)

• Propelling pencil

• General sewing supplies

• Quilter's wheel or quilter's ruler (optional)

NOTE: The original quilt has 2in pink borders at the top and bottom. These are not included in the quilt instructions. It is suggested that fabrics are 100 per cent cotton, 112cm (45in) wide, pre-washed and ironed. Instructions are given for hand-piecing.

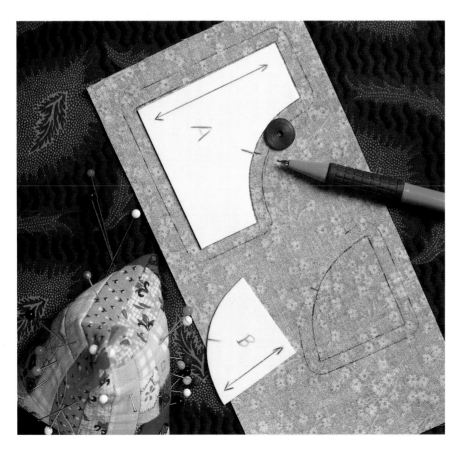

Step 1
Using the quilter's wheel to mark the seam allowance.

plain and print fabric, making sixteen A/B units for each block.

For each unit, take A, then place B on the underside with the right sides together. Place a pin through the curve at the matching point. Pin the sewing points on the outer corners, keeping the edges parallel with each other.

Place a pin either side of the centre pin, checking that the sewing lines match.

Step 2
Piecing the unit. i) Place B on A, pinning through the matching point on the curve. ii) Pin corners, keeping sides parallel. iii) The completed unit with seams pressed toward the darker fabric.

Step 3
The units joined into sections ready to piece together into the 10in block. Each section is turned a quarter-turn in a clockwise direction to make up the block.

Stitch along the curved sewing line with a small running stitch, starting and finishing with a back stitch (see Step 2). Press the units with the turnings towards the printed fabric.

To assemble each block, follow the sequence given in Step 3. Make four sections for each block. When you are sewing the sections together, turn each one a quarter-turn in a clockwise direction as shown.

Make another fifty-five blocks in the same manner.

ASSEMBLY

❖

Set the blocks out in eight rows with seven blocks across, so that they make a pleasing colour arrangement. Take a note of this order for later reference.

Sew the blocks together in rows, carefully matching the seams. Sew the horizontal rows together to complete the top of the quilt. Press the completed work with a hot iron.

BACKING

Cut the backing fabric in half across the width, then cut one width only in half lengthwise. Cut the selvedges off and sew a narrow width of fabric on either side of the full width of fabric. Using a hot iron, press all the seams open.

QUILTING

❖

The featured quilt has been quilted ⅛in away from each seam. Alternatively, mark in a quilting design of your choice.

Prepare the quilt top for basting by laying the backing with the wrong side up and smoothing it out. Place the batting on top, then centre the quilt top with the right side up. Pin or baste the three layers together and quilt through all thicknesses, working from the centre out.

FINISHING

❖

BINDING

Cut eight widths of binding fabric 2½in wide and join them together using bias joins to make one long length. Press the strip in half lengthwise with the wrong sides together.

With the raw edges of the quilt and binding together, attach the binding to the front of the quilt using ¼in seam allowance, sew through all thicknesses and mitre the corners.

Trim the excess batting and backing fabric, making sure that you leave sufficient to make a nice full binding.

Turn the binding to the back and slip stitch securely in place. Label and date the completed quilt.

BLOCK TEMPLATES

TEMPLATE B

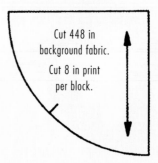

Cut 448 in
background fabric.

Cut 8 in print
per block.

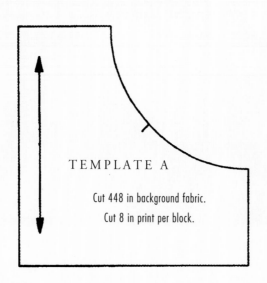

TEMPLATE A

Cut 448 in background fabric.

Cut 8 in print per block.

Add seam allowance to Template A and B

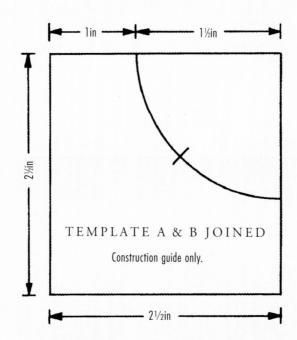

1in   1½in

2½in

TEMPLATE A & B JOINED

Construction guide only.

2½in

Floating Four-patch

An 1880s Floating Four-patch was the inspiration for this quilt in subtle shades reminiscent of days gone by. The original design has been adapted for machine piecing using one hundred and ninety-two colour-matched units.

FINISHED SIZE

- 150cm x 255cm (60in x 100in)
- Block size 12.5cm (5in) square

MATERIALS

Four-patches (made from 2in strips)

- 1.2m (1¹⁄₃yd) total assorted prints for the pale units. Choose mainly light fabrics but include a number of medium values as well

- 60cm (²⁄₃yd) total assorted prints in warm colours, pinks, reds, rusts, browns

- 60cm (²⁄₃yd) total assorted prints in cool colours, blues, greens, aquas, teals

Triangles

- 2.75m (3yd) fabrics in very light to light/medium values

- 1.5m (1³⁄₄yd) warm fabrics

- 1.5m (1³⁄₄yd) cool fabrics

- 5.2m (5³⁄₄yd) backing fabric

- 60cm (²⁄₃yd) binding fabric

- Batting to fit

- Thread to blend with all fabrics

- Thread for quilting, either machine or hand

- Rotary cutter, cutting mat, quilter's ruler, 16.5cm (6¹⁄₂in) quilter's square

- Sewing machine and general sewing supplies

NOTE: For the Four-patches, values should range from light/mediums through to darks. You should be able to cut at least one 2in strip from each fabric. For the triangles, values should range from light/medium to dark/mediums and include a few lights and brights. Choose a variety of print styles — small geometrics, tone-on-tone, lacy leaves and flowers, plaids, stripes, and small and large florals. It is best to have a balance of busy and calm fabrics. You should be able to cut at least two 4¹⁄₂in squares from each fabric.

Step 1
Cut pairs of 2in segments. Join the segments to make Four-patches.

PREPARATION

CUTTING

Four-patch fabrics

For the Four-patch fabrics, you will need a total of thirty strips. Cut twenty 2in strips to make up the light units and cut ten 2in strips each for the warm and cool units.

Triangle fabrics

Cut 4¹⁄₂in strips. You need twenty-two strips for the light units and eleven strips each for the warm and cool units.

Cut each of the strips into 4¹⁄₂in squares, then cut each square in half diagonally. You will need four triangles for each unit(see Diagram 1).

Binding fabric

Cut eight 2¹⁄₂in fabric strips for the binding.

CONSTRUCTION

NOTE: A ¹⁄₄in seam allowance is used throughout this pattern and is included in all measurements.

Sew all the 2in strips together into pairs and press the seams towards the darker fabric. Cut these sets into 2in

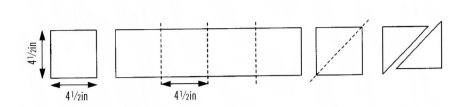

Diagram 1
Strips to squares to triangles.

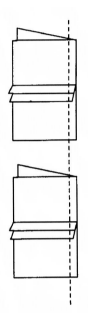

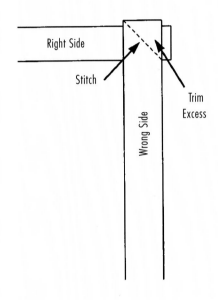

LIGHT	WARM	LIGHT	COOL
WARM	LIGHT	COOL	LIGHT
LIGHT	COOL	LIGHT	WARM
COOL	LIGHT	WARM	LIGHT

Diagram 2
Chain-sewing pieces.

Diagram 3
16-patch unit block.

Diagram 4
Join binding strips together with a 45° angle.

segments. Join these segments together into Four-patches. Save both time and thread by chain-piecing. Stitch the seam but do not cut the thread or lift the presser foot. Feed in the next piece as close as possible to the last and continue in the same manner until all the pieces are joined. Clip the threads between the pieces (see Diagram 2).

Chain-sew a triangle to one side of the Four-patch, then chain-sew the next triangle to the opposite side. Finger-press the seams towards the triangles.

Separate the units by cutting the joining threads. Add the two remaining triangles to the other side.

Trim the excess points from the seam allowance and press all the seams towards the triangles.

The units will have uneven outside

Step 2
Chain-sew the triangles to the opposite sides of the Four-patches.

Step 3
Chain-sew the triangles to the remaining sides and trim excess points.

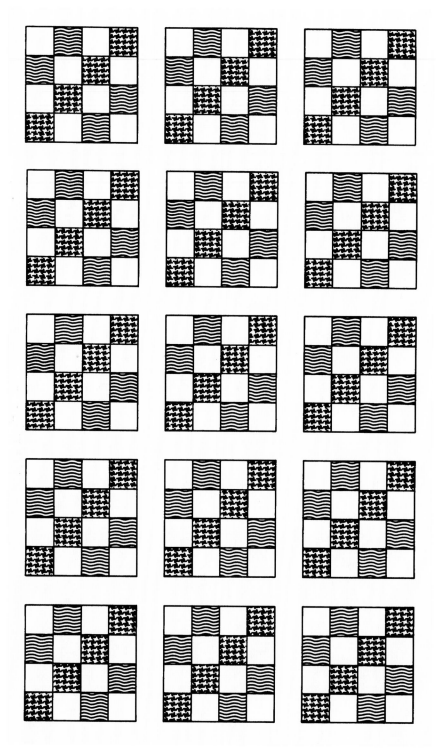

Block layout diagram

KEY

light

warm

cool

edges. Using a small quilter's square and rotary cutter, trim each unit to an exact and neat 5½in square.

You will need ninety-six light, forty-eight warm and forty-eight cool units.

ASSEMBLY

The quilt is best assembled as a series of sixteen unit blocks. Sew the units together using a mix of the light, cool and warm coloured units (pink, red, rusts and browns) as shown in Diagram 3. Sew these units together in five rows of three.

QUILTING

Cut the backing fabric in half and join each half together along the long sides. Sandwich the quilt top, batting and backing and baste the three layers together. Machine or hand quilt as desired. This quilt has been hand quilted inside each small square and triangle shape.

FINISHING

BINDING

Trim away the excess batting and backing. Join the binding strips together at a 45 degree angle to make one long strip and press in half lengthwise, wrong sides together (see Diagram 4).

With raw edges together, sew the binding to the front of the quilt through all thicknesses.

Mitre the corners as you sew. Turn the binding to the back of the quilt and slip stitch the edge to the backing fabric.

Sign and date your quilt.

My Favourite Flannel Quilt

*Wonderfully warm and beautifully soft, this quilt
was designed and made in double-brushed flannel fabrics.
The simple pattern enhances the mellow charm
and irresistible cuddliness of the flannel.*

TERMS USED

Nub. To nub right-angled triangles, place your ruler so that the line denoting the finished size of the square plus ¹⁄₂in is on the short side of the triangle. Using a rotary cutter, cut off the ¹⁄₄in point which protrudes beyond the right hand edge of the ruler. Repeat for the second side. This facilitates piecing and removes the excess fabric from the intersections of the piecing. This is vital with a thicker fabric such as flannel, but also creates neater work with any fabric.

PREPARATION

CUTTING

From each of the two main fabrics for the centre pieced panel, cut twelve 5⁷⁄₈in squares. Cut each square in half diagonally and nub ¹⁄₄in. From each of the other fabrics selected for the centre pieced section, cut two 5⁷⁄₈in squares. Cut in half diagonally and again nub ¹⁄₄in.

CONSTRUCTION

ASSEMBLY

Centre

You will need to make twelve blocks. Sew the triangles together in pairs. You should have two bias squares with the first main fabric (M1) and one of the other fabrics, and two bias squares with the second main fabric (M2) and one of the other fabrics. Arrange each block as shown.

First border

Cut four 3in strips from the first border fabric. It is not necessary to join the fabric for these strips, they can be cut from selvedge to selvedge. You will need two strips each 3in x 30¹⁄₂in for the top and bottom of the quilt and two pieces each 3in x 40¹⁄₂in for the sides of the quilt. You will also need four 3in squares from the outer border fabric for each of the corners.

Join one strip to each side of the quilt. Join one 3in square to each end of the two remaining border strips. Join these to the top and bottom of the quilt.

Trapezium border

Cut three 5¹⁄₂in strips from each of the two fabrics. Using the template provided, cut twenty-two trapezium shapes from the first fabric and eighteen from the second fabric.

Make two border strips with nine trapeziums. Alternate the two colours beginning and ending with the first fabric (top and bottom borders). Make two border strips with eleven trapeziums. Alternate the two colours beginning and ending with the first fabric (side borders).

Measure the top of the quilt and divide the length in half. Fold the top and bottom border strip in half and trim to this size. It is important that this measurement be taken from the centre of the middle trapezium. Repeat this step with the side borders. Add a 5¹⁄₂in square of the outer border fabric to each end of the two side border strips.

Sew the top and bottom borders to the quilt first, then sew the two side border strips.

FINISHED SIZE

- 152cm x 178cm (60in x 70in)

MATERIALS

- 45cm (¹⁄₂yd) each of two main fabrics for the centre pieced panel
- 60cm (²⁄₃yd) each of two fabrics for second (trapezium) border
- 25cm (¹⁄₃yd) each of 12 other fabrics for centre pieced panel and squares border
- 1m (1¹⁄₈yd) for first border and binding
- 4.5m (5yd) for outer border and quilt backing
- Twenty-four old buttons at least 1.5cm (⁵⁄₈in) diameter
- 20cm (¹⁄₄yd) Vliesofix or Wonderunder for appliqué
- Batting

M1 = First main fabric
M2 = Second main fabric

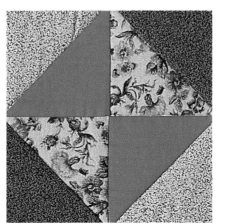

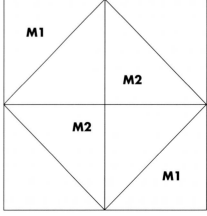

fabrics on the marked line with scissors, remove the backing paper and position them on the quilt top. Iron in place with a hot dry iron. Use either a Running Stitch or Blanket Stitch or a combination of both to topstitch around the shapes.

BACKING

Piece the remaining backing pieces so that your backing layer is 2in bigger than the quilt top on all sides. Place the backing layer right side down.

Cut the batting to the same size as the backing and lay it over the backing piece. Batting which has been rolled and packed in a bag should be taken out of its wrapper and laid out overnight on a bed or on a large flat surface to 'rest' so that any heavy creasing can be minimised.

Place the quilt top right side up and centred over the batting and backing. Pin or baste as preferred.

QUILTING

❖

This quilt is suitable for tying or machine quilting. The sample quilt has been quilted around the triangles in the central pieced area, then around each border and finally around the hearts. Buttons can also be sewn into alternate trapezium shapes in this border.

FINISHING

❖

BINDING

As this is a fairly thick quilt, the finished size of the binding should be at least ½in all the way around. To achieve this size, it is necessary to cut the binding 3in wide.

Sign and date your quilt.

Third border

Cut eighty-four 3in squares from a variety of the fabrics (excluding the two previous border fabrics and the outer border fabric). Join them to make two strips, each with eighteen squares and attach these to the top and bottom of the quilt. Join two strips with twenty-four squares and attach them to the sides of the quilt.

Take care where these borders 'turn' the corner so no one fabric is repeated in the adjoining squares.

Outer border

Cut two 5½in strips of fabric for the outer border. These can be cut in one length parallel to the selvedge and the backing for the quilt can be pieced from the remaining fabric. For the top and bottom of the quilt, the strips should measure 5½in x 50in. For the sides of the quilt the strips should measure 5½in x 70½in. Join the strips to the top and bottom of the quilt, press, then join the strips to the sides of the quilt. Press.

APPLIQUÉ

❖

Using the template provided, trace fourteen hearts onto the backing paper of the Vliesofix. Cut roughly around each heart leaving the drawn line intact. Press these onto your chosen fabrics. Cut out the

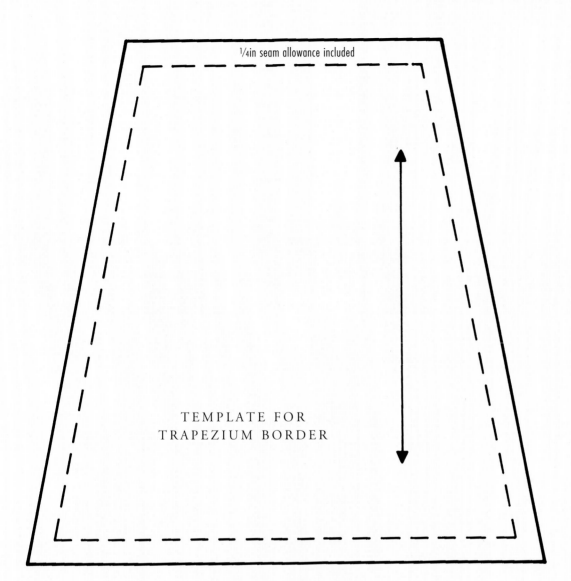

¼in seam allowance included

TEMPLATE FOR
TRAPEZIUM BORDER

HEART TEMPLATE

HELPFUL HINT

When using flannel fabrics there are several things that need to be kept in mind. Choose a design that has relatively large individual pieces. In this design there is no piece smaller than 2½in. Flannel is a heavier weight than the usual patchwork cottons so the seams are bulkier. If the pattern is too complex this could create a problem.

When cutting flannel with a rotary cutter it is important to clean the blades regularly as fluff builds up between the blade and the guard and prevents efficient cutting.

 SS

Highways and Byways

Jacob's Ladder Block has always been an old favourite. This wonderful quilt
is a little different with highways and byways running diagonally across it.
The end result may look complicated but the piecing is relatively easy.
It's the colour combination which adds much of the interest.

PREPARATION

CUTTING

NOTE: All cutting instructions include ¼in seam allowance. Strips are cut across the full width of the fabric unless otherwise indicated.

From the green button print, cut four 2in wide strips for the Four-patch squares. Cut three 3⅞in wide strips for the half-square triangles.

From the red button print, cut the same strips as above.

From the white button print, cut six 9½in wide strips for the plain blocks. Cross-cut these strips into 9½in squares. A total of twenty-four squares is required. Cut seven 3½in wide strips for the first border.

From the red check print, cut seven 2in wide strips for the Four-patch squares for both the blocks and outer border. Cut eight 2¼in wide strips for binding.

From the green check print, cut seven 2in wide strips for the Four-patch squares for both the blocks and for the outer border.

From the beige print, cut ten 2in wide strips to make up the Four-patch squares.

Cut six 3⅞in wide strips for the half-square triangles.

CONSTRUCTION

PIECING

In each Jacob's Ladder Block there are four button print Half-square triangles, three button print Four-patch squares and two check print Four-patch squares.

Join two strips lengthwise, cross-cut into 2in pieces and reassemble to form the Four-patch squares.

Four-patch squares

Join a 2in strip of beige print to a 2in strip of green button print along the longest edge of the strips. Press with the seam towards the green prints. Cross-cut the strip into 2in pieces. Repeat using three strips each of beige and green prints. Stitch units together with opposing colours in each corner and butting seams together.

Repeat these steps using four strips of beige print and four strips of 2in red button print. You will require thirty-six Four-patch squares in each colour way of both red and green button prints.

The red check and green check Four-patch squares are made in the same manner but twenty-four of each colour way Four-patch squares are required.

Use three strips of red check print, three strips of green check print and six strips of 2in beige print. Save the leftover Four-patch squares for the outer border.

FINISHED SIZE

- 213cm x 167cm (84in x 66in)
- Block size 23cm (9in) square

MATERIALS

- 60cm (⅔yd) green button print
- 60cm (⅔yd) red button print
- 2.1m (2⅓yd) white button print
- 1.2m (1⅓yd) red check print
- 55cm (⅝yd) green check print
- 4.8m (5⅓yd) backing fabric
- 2.1m (2⅓yd) beige print
- Sufficient batting to fit
- Rotary cutter, ruler and mat
- Neutral thread
- Sewing machine and general sewing supplies
- Thread for quilting

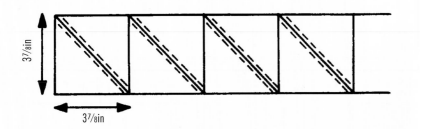

Diagram 1
On the reverse side of each of the 3⅞in beige print strips mark fine pencil lines at 3⅞in intervals. Mark a diagonal line through each of the squares.

Half-square triangles

On the reverse side of each of the 3⅞in beige print strips, mark fine pencil lines at 3⅞in intervals. Mark a diagonal line through each of the squares (see Diagram 1). With right sides together, place a 3⅞in strip of green button fabric and the marked beige fabric together and stitch a ¼in seam on either side of the drawn diagonal line. After stitching, cut through each square and also on the diagonal pencil line. Press squares open with the seam towards the darker fabric. Repeat these steps with beige fabric and green button print. You will need forty-eight Half-square triangles in each colour way.

Jacob's Ladder Block

Using both the Four-patch squares and the Half-square triangles, piece together a Jacob's Ladder Block in rows of three (see Diagram 2). When stitching the three rows together to complete each block, ensure that the points meet and press each row in alternating directions. This helps when butting the seams together and keeps the block flat. Refer to the colour photograph for colour placement. The green and red button fabric ladders run in diagonal rows across the quilt, with the green and red check Four-patch squares making the byways through the other diagonal line of the quilt. Join Jacob's Ladder and plain blocks together. There are six blocks across and eight blocks down in our quilt. Again, press the seams in each row in opposing

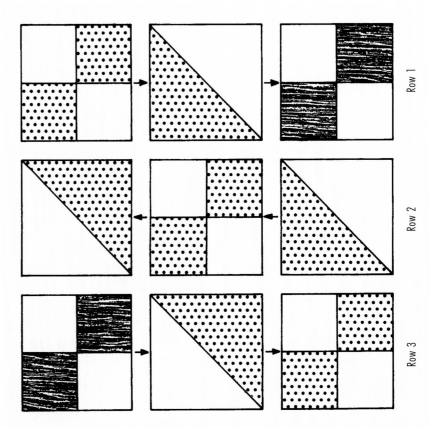

Row 1

Row 2

Row 3

Diagram 2
Using both your Four-patch squares and Half-square triangles piece together a Jacob's Ladder Block in rows of three.

directions. Sew the eight rows together to make the quilt top and press with a hot iron across the entire quilt.

BORDERS

For the first border, measure the length of the quilt and stitch the previously cut 3½in white button borders to either side of the quilt top. It will be necessary to join strips to make up the lengths required. Press and measure through the centre of the quilt to determine the width. Attach the upper and lower borders as before and press.

For the second border, make a total of ninety-six red and green Four-patch squares (forty-eight in each colour way) using the remaining 2in wide strips. Don't forget to use those left over from the Jacob's Ladder Blocks.

Commencing with a green and beige Four-patch square, join twenty-six units together and attach to the left-hand side of the quilt. Repeat this for the right-hand side of the quilt starting this time with a red and beige unit. Press seams towards the first border. Use twenty-two Four-patch squares for the top and bottom borders, rotating the units so that the colours alternate at the beginning of each border. Press.

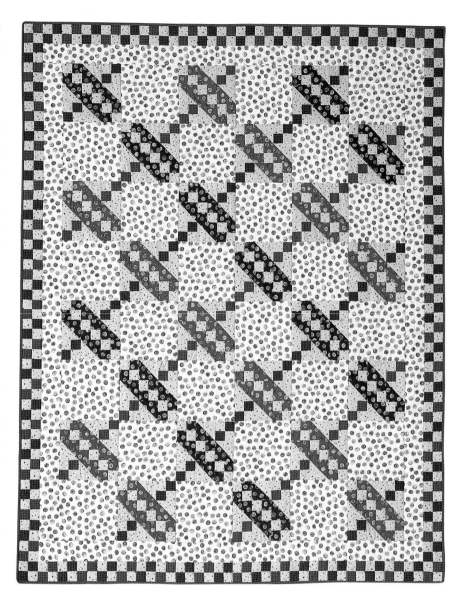

QUILTING

Cut the 5⅓yd piece of backing fabric into two lengths of 2⅔yd. Join these pieces along one long edge to make the backing piece.

Layer the quilt top, batting and backing fabric and pin or baste. The plain 9in blocks are a wonderful space to display hand or machine quilting. The sample block was machine quilted in the ditch around all of the units comprising the Jacob's Ladder blocks, as well as free machine quilted in the plain blocks.

FINISHING

BINDING

Join the eight 2¼in red check strips together using 45 degree seams. Press these in half with the wrong sides together.

Align the raw edges of the binding with the raw edges of the front of the quilt. Stitch ¼in from the edge through all three layers of the quilt and the binding. Trim away the excess backing and batting. Roll the binding to the back of the quilt and hand stitch it in place.

Label and date your quilt.

Virginia Reel

*There's a naive quality about this vibrant scrap quilt. The Virginia Reel
Block features stripes, plaids, florals and plains in the distinctive
eight-pointed star. Hand-pieced, probably in the 1950s,
it includes dress and shirt fabrics as well as furnishing scraps.*

To reproduce this style, use a contrasting mix of prints and avoid using too many small-print fabrics. Study the photograph to assist with your colour choices. The mix of yellow, pink, brown, purple, red and blue all contribute to the overall rustic feel of this quilt and the effect is pulled together with the use of plain yellow squares and brown border. The quilter has used a double thread for the quilting design, which emphasises the stitches and gives the whole quilt a rustic theme.

The Virginia Reel Blocks in the original quilt are pieced together with a full yellow square between each block. These instructions have triangles in each corner as the block would be made traditionally.

PREPARATION

CUTTING

From the length of the yellow fabric, cut two strips at 1¾in x 87in and two at 1¾in x 60½in, set these aside for the borders.

Use the remaining yellow fabric for the C triangles.

From the brown fabric, cut eight strips 2¼in wide by the width of the fabric, put this aside for the binding.

Put aside the remaining brown fabric for the backing and binding.

Each fat quarter should yield approxi-

mately eight A outer diamonds, eight B squares and eight D star diamonds for the blocks.

Carefully trace and cut out the templates provided. Note that template A and D are identical diamonds with different grainlines, so be sure to use the correct one where necessary.

Working on the wrong side of the fabric and taking care with grain placement, trace around the templates with the 2B pencil. The templates are the finished size, so add a ¼in seam allowance around each one when cutting out. Mark each template with its name and grainline.

For each block you will need

From the fat quarters, cut eight As, eight Bs, and eight Ds. These will be mixed amongst the blocks.

NOTE: D is the star template and two different fabrics are used for D in each block.

From the yellow fabric, cut four Cs.

CONSTRUCTION

This quilt requires a total of thirty-five Virginia Reel Blocks.

First select your fabric combinations. For each block choose four of the D diamonds in one print and four of the D diamonds in a contrasting print for the star points. Select eight of the B squares in one fabric and eight of the A diamonds in one fabric for the outer ring around the star. You will also need four yellow C triangles.

Pinning and stitching of the eight-pointed star is important to produce a flat block. Pin at either end and in the centre of each seam, carefully aligning the drawn lines on both sides, before you begin stitching. Take a small back stitch every fifth or sixth stitch to give extra strength to the seam.

FINISHED SIZE

- 159cm x 220cm (62½in x 86½in)
- Block size 30cm (12in)

MATERIALS

- 35 fat quarters or a large range of scrap fabrics for the star blocks. Four different scrap fabrics are required for each block
- 2.5m (2¾yd) yellow fabric
- 5.2m (5¾yd) brown fabric for backing and binding
- 178cm x 239cm (70in x 94in) batting
- Template plastic
- 2B pencil
- Neutral sewing thread (grey or beige)
- Quilting thread

NOTE: It is suggested that fabrics be 100 per cent cotton, 112cm (45in) wide, prewashed and ironed. It is desirable to have a sizeable mix of prints to achieve the naive effect. If you wish to replicate the look of this quilt, try to incorporate some prints that resemble dress fabrics in appearance. Carefully study the photograph of the quilt to assist with colour choices — the mix of yellow, pink, brown, purple, red and blue all contribute to the overall feel of the quilt.

Virginia Reel block construction

the centre of the block, where the eight seams come together.

Halfway down the seam between the D pieces, gradually stitch below the marked line as shown in Diagram 2, so you have tapered in by about $1/16$in when you've reached the end.

HELPFUL HINT

Tapering the stitches toward the centre intersection reduces bulk and assists the block to lie smoothly in the centre.

This completes a star section. Repeat for three more B squares, ensuring that the D fabrics are in the identical order.

To set in the four remaining B squares, refer to Diagram 2. Pin and stitch a star section to one side of a B square. Then pin and stitch a second star section to the other side of the square. Lastly, pin and stitch the two Ds. Remember to taper the seam as it approaches the centre. Complete the other half of the star in the same manner.

Complete the star by pinning one of the last two B squares into place on the lower half of the block, then the upper section to B, finally stitching and tapering towards the centre. Pin and stitch the last B to the other side in the same manner.

Referring to Diagram 1 showing the set-in square technique, pin and stitch a D diamond to the side of a B square. Then pin and stitch a contrasting D to the adjacent side of B. Lastly, pin and stitch the seam between the two Ds, commencing at the corner of B and working down. This seam is travelling towards

Diagram 1
Joining the B squares to the D diamonds.

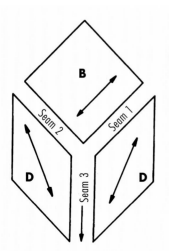

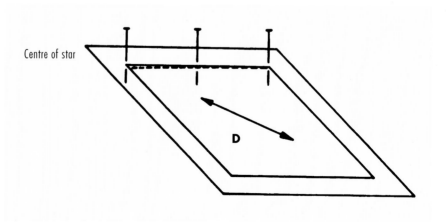

Diagram 2
Stitching towards the centre of the star.

Diagram 3
Virginia Reel Block layout.

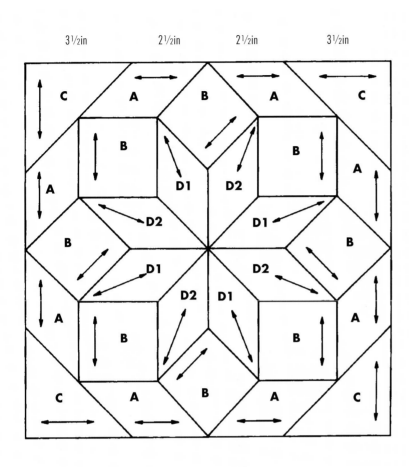

3½in   2½in   2½in   3½in

Now that the centre star is completed, press all of the D seams in the one direction, spiralling them around the central point of the star. This helps to keep the block flat.

Press the seams on the upper edges of D pieces towards the B square.

Referring to the block layout diagram and the step-by-step photograph, ensure correct placement for the A diamond round. Pin and stitch each A to the outer edges of the Bs. Take care to pin the set-in point of A directly above the star point.

Press the seams toward A.

Fold the C triangles in half along the long edge and finger-press to crease at the centre. Match the centre of C to the seam intersection between the D diamonds and the point of the B square. Pin and stitch each of the corner Cs in place. Press toward C.

ASSEMBLY

Referring to the quilt layout diagram, set the blocks out in seven rows of five across. Move the blocks around until they are in a pleasing colour arrangement.

Sew the blocks together in rows, carefully matching and pinning each intersection as you go.

Press each row in alternate directions; rows 1, 3, 5, and 7 towards the left and rows 2, 4, and 6 towards the right. This helps the seams at the intersections to butt each other together more firmly. Sew the rows to each other, carefully aligning and pinning seam intersections.

YELLOW BORDER

Using the two 60½in strips of fabric set aside for the border, fold them in half to determine the centre point and pin them to the top and bottom borders. Sew and press towards the borders. Using the remaining 87in strips, use the same method to attach to both sides. Press the seams towards the borders.

BACKING

Fold the backing fabric in half, right sides together, aligning the raw edges opposite the fold.

Beginning at the raw edge, sew along the selvedges of the right-hand side, towards the fold, with an ½in seam. Trim off the selvedge.

Cut the fold open so that you have a backing piece with a centre seam. Press the seam open.

QUILTING

Press the pieced top and pieced backing firmly. Lay out the backing with the wrong side up and the seam running up and down and smooth out the wrinkles. Centre the batting on top and smooth it out, then centre the pieced top, right

side up. Baste the quilt in a grid pattern, at approximately 5in intervals.

Roll the excess batting and backing to the edge of the quilt and baste to hold securely while quilting.

The original Virginia Reel quilt was hand quilted using a double strand of regular sewing thread, which gives the quilting the appearance of quilting thread we use today. The quilting pattern is a corner grid design which does not follow the block design and may have been stitched from the back.

Once the quilting is complete, remove the basting threads and lay the quilt out on a smooth surface. Carefully trim the edges of the batting and backing to align with the edges of the pieced top. Check that all corners are square, square off and trim if necessary.

FINISHING

BINDING

Although the quilt top has been hand pieced, it is recommended to sew the binding to the quilt by machine to ensure strength through all the layers.

Using the eight 2¼in wide strips, sew them together with bias seams. Press seams open.

Fold the strip with right sides out. Set the machine to a slighter longer stitch length than normal.

Align all the raw edges and sew with a generous ¼in seam allowance.

Turn the binding to the back of the quilt and hand sew in place.

Label and date your quilt.

Virginia Reel quilt layout.

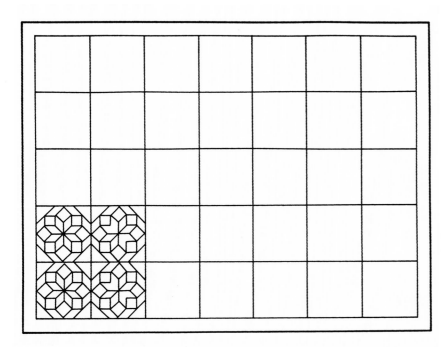

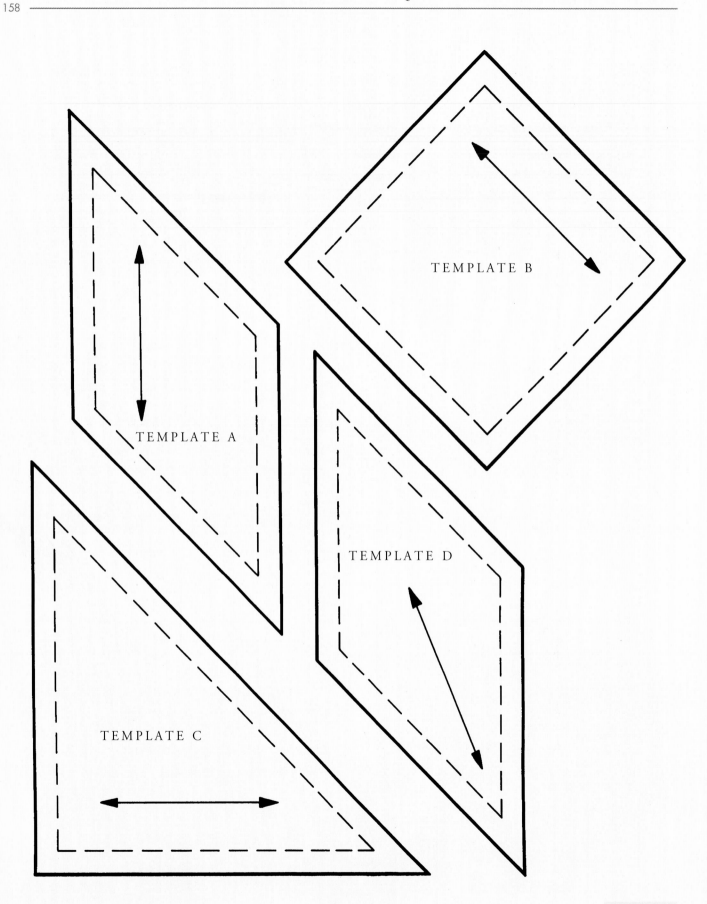

TEMPLATE A

TEMPLATE B

TEMPLATE C

TEMPLATE D

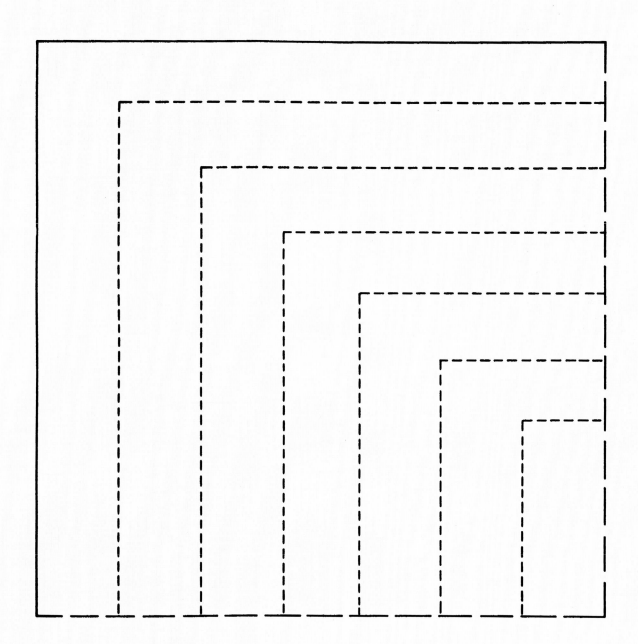

QUILTING PATTERN FOR 12in BLOCK
(Half Scale)

Basic Equipment

KEY

1	Paper Cutting Scissors	**8**	Needles	**15**	Rotary Cutter
2	Dressmakers' Scissors	**9**	HB Pencil	**16**	100% Cotton Thread
3	Embroidery Scissors	**10**	Silver Marking Pencil	**17**	Cotton/Polyester Thread
4	Tape Measure	**11**	Templates	**18**	Cutting Mat
5	Thimble	**12**	Glass Headed Pins	**19**	Safety Pins
6	Ruby Beholder	**13**	Plastic Ruler		
7	Adjustable Ruler	**14**	Pin Cushion		

BASIC EQUIPMENT

We may have come a long way since quilts were first made in the 1880s, but the basic tools for patchwork such as needles, thread, pins and scissors remain the essentials.

NEEDLES

For machine stitching you will need a supply of new sewing machine needles for light to medium-weight cottons.

A 'betweens' needle is considered the best for both hand piecing and quilting. 'Sharps' are used when a longer needle is required. A good general rule is to use as fine a needle as you can manage comfortably; size 8 is recommended for beginners. If you want to make smaller stitches as you progress, use a smaller needle. Size 12 is the smallest.

THREAD

Traditionally, synthetic threads are used with synthetic fabrics and cotton with cotton fabrics. Polyester-cotton thread (polyester core wrapped in cotton) or 100 per cent cotton thread are best for cotton fabrics and are the easiest to use for all other fabrics. This thread does have a tendency to fray and tangle so avoid this by knotting the end before unrolling the thread, then cutting and threading the other end through the needle.

Select a colour that matches the darkest fabric you are sewing. If you are using different fabrics, select a neutral thread such as grey or ecru which will blend inconspicuously with all of them.

PINS

Glass-headed pins are very sharp and good for piercing straight through the material when lining up a seam or a starting point.

There is a longer pin available which is excellent for pinning together layers on more bulky projects.

SCISSORS

You will need three pairs of scissors for patchwork. Dressmaker's shears, preferably with a bent handle – these should be extremely sharp and used only for cutting fabric. Paper scissors – never cut paper with sewing shears, as this will dull the blades. Embroidery scissors for clipping threads and seam allowances – these should also be very sharp.

ROTARY CUTTER AND MAT

A rotary cutter is an excellent tool for cutting strips, straightening fabric edges and cutting out a variety of geometric patchwork pieces. It also enables more accurate cutting of several layers of fabric at once.

Choose a cutter with a large blade, and keep spare blades handy. Always cut on a mat specially designed for a rotary cutter to keep the blade sharp. Fold the fabric in half on the mat with right sides facing and selvedges matching. The drafting triangle sits directly on the fold of the fabric, the rotary rule sits on the left edge of the triangle. The mat grips the fabric and helps the blade to cut straight. A 'self-healing' cutting mat is ideal.

RULERS

A long, clear plastic ruler is a must to use with a rotary cutter. These rulers are well marked and sturdy and there is no danger of shaving off a piece of the ruler when cutting layers of fabric.

PENCILS

A soft lead pencil is the traditional option for marking a design, but there is also a variety of marking pencils available. Probably the most useful is a water soluble pencil, as it gradually fades after a period of time.

Be careful, however, as the design is liable to disappear before the project can be finished.

TEMPLATES

Templates can be homemade from graph paper, tracing paper and cardboard or template plastic. The edges of cardboard templates tend to wear after frequent cutting of patches, but plastic and metal templates, which are available in a great variety of shapes and sizes, are virtually indestructible. This is a great advantage, especially for a large project which requires cutting out several of each shape.

Window templates are useful if you are featuring or centring a motif or flower in a patch.

Templates for hand sewing, appliqué and quilting are cut to the exact shape without seam allowance. They mark the stitching line not the cutting line. For machine sewing, include 6mm (1/4in) seam allowance around all edges.

THIMBLES

A thimble is indispensable if you are quilting by hand. It is also good to use on the finger underneath the work to push the needle back through the fabric.

FRAMES AND HOOPS

A frame or a hoop makes the quilting of large projects, such as bed-sized quilts, much easier. It is not essential to use one for smaller items, but you will get a better finish.

FABRICS

Choosing the most suitable fabric for your patchwork project is important, especially for a beginner. Some fabrics are easier to work with than others. With experience, you will discover which fabric is a joy to use and which is an absolute headache. The most important rules to remember are to buy the best fabric you can afford. A firmly woven, lightweight, 100 per cent pure cotton which is easier to use, lasts longer and gives crisp results.

Synthetics and mixtures can be difficult to iron and handle and may pucker along the seams but they are attractive, versatile and can be unusual or striking in appearance. They are often more readily available than 100 per cent cottons, but they are not all easier to use. Some tend to be slippery, floppy and soft.

As you gain experience, you may want to experiment with more exotic fabrics. Many of these will need special handling but to find out about these fabrics, you will have to test them yourself. Some satins and taffeta can be too fragile for patchwork. Synthetics also tend to be more difficult to quilt through as they are slightly spongy.

COLOURS AND PRINTS

The successful combining of colours is often a matter of trial and error, not something that can be taught. The only way to find out if it will work is by trying it.

To achieve a good contrast, you need a mix of prints: small, medium, large, checks, stripes and plains. A mix of colours is also important. Contrast rather than coordinate. You will need a mixture of colour values – twenty per cent darks, forty per cent mediums and forty per cent lights is a good mix.

The value, or the lightness or darkness of a colour is probably more important than the actual colour when you are making a quilt. To achieve successful results, try to use a range of values.

Many small-scale floral prints are available. Although a safe choice, they are sometimes so safe and well colour-coordinated that they give a rather dull and uninspired finished effect.

Experiment with prints of varying scale, stripes and border designs, geometric prints and checks. Some large-scale prints can introduce a delicate, lacy effect. Take particular care with stripes. If they are not cut and sewn perfectly straight, it will be very obvious.

Certain fabrics are evocative of different eras or styles. Create a country-style quilt by including fabrics which are bold and brightly coloured and include different-sized checks, stripes, ticking, stars and geometric prints.

A 1930s style quilt can be created by including fabrics such as bright pastels, fresh florals, perky checks, stripes and white backgrounds.

FABRICS TO AVOID

Stretch fabrics such as knits and some crepes should always be avoided. Very closely woven fabrics can also prove difficult, even for machine sewing. This applies to heavy fabrics such as canvas, and lightweight fabrics like some poplins.

Very open weave fabrics can cause difficulties with fraying and with their transparency.

PREPARATION OF FABRICS

Always wash your fabrics before use. This will pre-shrink them, remove excess dye and remove any sizing, so that the fabric is easier to handle. Machine wash your fabrics unless you have only a small quantity of fabric.

The volume of water used for washing seems to flush the dye and sizing out thoroughly. It is unusual to have a problem such as the dye running from one fabric to others, but if you are not sure of a fabric, always hand wash it separately.

If tumble drying, a short drying time is quite sufficient, unless the pieces are very large.

Don't over-dry fabrics, as they may become very creased. Remove while they are still slightly damp, then iron them.

When you are purchasing batting for your quilt, it is important to read the washing instructions before you make your choice. Some synthetic battings are often unsuitable for ordinary laundering. Always choose natural fibre battings such as wool, cotton or silk. A good mixture is 90 per cent cotton and 10 per cent polyester. This blend is suitable for both hand and machine quilting and it also washes very well.

Conversion Chart for Fabrics

In that cupboard full of treasured fabrics that every dedicated quilter owns, there are special favourites that are only 90cm wide, when you need 115cm or 150cm width for a special project. Our chart below will show you how to convert the fabric to the width you need.

WIDTH	90cm	115cm	150cm
MEASUREMENT	1.6m	1.3m	0.9m
	1.8m	1.5m	1.1m
	2.1m	1.6m	1.3m
	2.3m	1.9m	1.5m
	2.6m	2.1m	1.6m
	2.9m	2.3m	1.7m
	3.1m	2.5m	1.8m
	3.4m	2.6m	2.1m
	3.9m	2.9m	2.2m
	4.1m	3.1m	2.4m
	4.3m	3.3m	2.5m
	4.6m	3.5m	2.6m

If one of your favourite fabrics is 90cm wide and the size you require is 2.5m x 115cm, go down to the 2.5m in the 115cm column and directly across to the 90cm column. You will need 3.1m of the 90cm fabric for the same project. Remember to allow a little more for napped fabric.

Basic Instructions

Patchwork quilts can be made in many different ways. Here we give you the basic techniques required to successfully complete a quilt.

DESIGN AND DRAFTING

To adapt a design or border, or see how the quilt will look and fit together, you will need to make a sketch on graph paper.

Graph paper is used for two things – to make small sketches of quilt designs (graph plan) and to make full size drawings of shapes for templates or as guides for rotary cutting.

You can play with different colourings with a graph plan and use it as a reference map as you construct your quilt. This helps to see the relative proportions of the border and quilt and to judge the effect. A sketch also lets you preview your quilt and make improvements before you start cutting and sewing.

A quilt sketch is a drawing of the quilt in miniature. You will need to assign a scale in order to calculate the finished size of the quilt and to draft templates. Keep the scale easy so that cutting dimensions will match standard markings on your rotary cutting ruler.

DRAFTING TEMPLATES

Graph paper marked in ¼in is one of the easiest to use to make full size drawings of template shapes. You can draw a full size block or portion of a border onto graph paper and identify each shape to be cut by lightly colouring it in, then add a consistent ¼in seam allowance around each one. Trace the completed shapes onto template material or use the

measurements as cutting guides for template-free rotary cutting.

Template plastic with a ¼in grid is also available, so that shapes can be drawn directly onto it and an accurate seam allowance added. If the templates are to be used for machine sewing, add a ¼in seam allowance all around. If the template is being used for hand sewing, add a ¼in seam allowance when cutting out the fabric. Straight grain arrows should be marked onto templates.
NOTE: The outside edges of a block or quilt must always be on the straight grain, or the quilt will not lie flat. Mark your graphed blocks and borders accordingly.

Glueing a piece of sandpaper to the back of a paper or plastic template, with the gritty side facing down, is a great way of cutting accurate shapes from fabric.

Standard Template

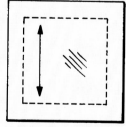

Machine Sewing Template

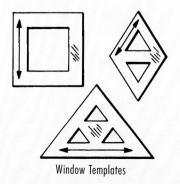

Window Templates

The sandpaper adds weight and sturdiness and the rough surface grips the fabric for more accurate cutting.
NOTE: Do not cut your sandpaper with fabric scissors

CUTTING

Trim the selvedge from the fabric before you begin. If you are using one fabric for both borders and block pieces, cut the borders first, then the block pieces from what is left over.

Position the templates on the fabric so that the arrows match the straight grain of the fabric. With a sharp pencil (an erasable pencil or a white for dark fabrics, or lead pencil for light fabrics), trace around the template on the fabric. Allow a further ¼in all around the drawn shape for seam allowance before cutting out. Templates for machine sewing usually include a seam allowance, but these pieces must be precisely cut as there is no drawn line to guide your sewing. Multiple layers can be cut at the one time by folding and pressing the fabric into layers before placing the template. Make sure that each piece is cut on the straight grain.

ROTARY OR TEMPLATE-FREE CUTTING

It is important to use the rotary cutter accurately and efficiently to ensure straight pieces. Straighten the fabric by folding it in layers, selvedge to selvedge to fit on the cutting mat. Lay a triangle along the folded edge of the fabric and push it against the right side of the ruler until it is just at the edge.

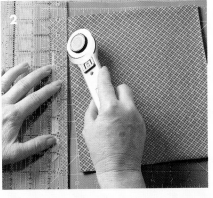

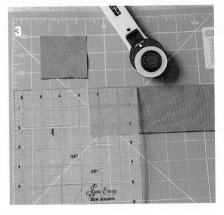

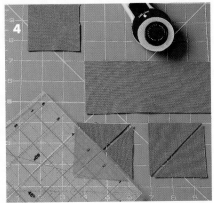

right sides together, so the marked seam line on the wrong side of the fabric is visible on both sides of the patchwork when sewing. Sew the seam through the pencilled lines with a short running stitch and occasional back stitch, using a single thread.

Begin and end each seam at the seam line (not at the edge of fabric) with two or three back stitches to secure the seam and sew from point to point, not edge to edge.

When joining the blocks and the rows together, do not sew the seam allowance down. Sew up to the dot marking the corner, then begin on the next side by taking a couple of extra small back stitches and continue sewing along the line. This leaves your options open as to which way to press the seam allowance when the block is completed.

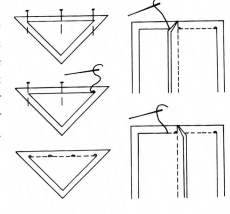

Hold the ruler down with your left hand, remove the triangle and begin cutting. Walk your hand up parallel with the cutter and continue to cut off the end of the fabric. Do not try to hold the ruler at the bottom as you will most likely move it.

Once you have straightened the fabric, use the cutter and ruler to cut strips of fabric to the width you require.

Squares, rectangles and triangles are all cut from strips. Remember when cutting squares and rectangles to add ½in to the desired finished measurement. For a 2in finished square cut a 2½in square. For a 2in x 4in finished rectangle, cut 2½in x 4½in.

Half square triangles are half a square with the short sides on the straight grain and the long side on the bias. To cut these triangles, cut a square in half diagonally. Cut the square ⅞in larger than the finished short side of the triangle to allow for seam allowances.

Quarter square triangles are used along the outside edge of a quilt

and some blocks are quarter square triangles. These triangles have their short sides on the bias and the long side on the straight grain. These triangles are cut from squares. Each square is cut into four on the diagonal and each is 1¼in larger than the finished long side of the triangle.

PIECING METHODS

❖

Hand piecing

Pieces for hand piecing require precisely marked seam lines; marked cutting lines are optional. Place the template face down on the wrong side of the fabric and draw around it accurately with a sharp pencil. Leave space between patches for a ¼in seam allowance when cutting.

After marking the patches, cut outward from the seam line ¼in, measuring the distance by eye. Join the pieces

ENGLISH PAPER PIECING METHOD

❖

This hand piecing technique involves basting fabric over a thin cardboard or paper template. The shapes are stitched together to form blocks and ultimately to form a quilt. Although time-consuming, this method results in precise, sharp seams and a professional finished appearance. It also has the advantage of being able to be picked up, put down and carried around.

When hand piecing over paper, cut out an exact sized light cardboard template for every pattern piece, as well as a cardboard pattern for every piece. Cut out the fabric shape using the cardboard pattern and include ¼in seam allowance all around.

Place the cardboard template in the centre of the wrong side of the fabric shape. Working one side at a time, fold over the seam allowance onto the template. Baste into place through the template, making sure the corners of the fabric are neatly folded in. For easy

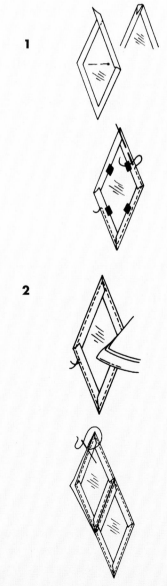

removal of the basting, start with a knot and finish with a simple double stitch.

To join the patches together, place them right sides facing and match corners. With a matching thread, or a mid-grey thread which blends with most colours, join the edges from corner to corner using a tiny Whip Stitch and double stitch the corners. The stitch should be fairly small and not visible from the right side of the fabric. Make each block separately by sewing the smallest pieces together first to form units. Join smaller units to form larger ones until the block is complete. Press, then join the blocks together to form rows and the rows together to form the sampler or quilt top.

The cardboard templates can be removed when all the pieces are joined together. Turn the quilt over, press well with a warm iron and allow to cool. Carefully remove the basting stitches and lift out each piece of cardboard separately.

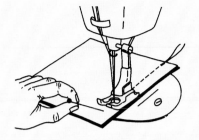

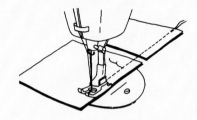

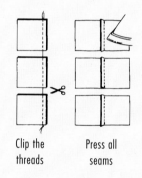

Clip the threads

Press all seams

MACHINE PIECING

❖

Accurate cutting is very important especially in machine piecing. Include seam allowances in the template and mark the cutting line on the back of the fabric.

Use white or neutral thread as light in colour as the lightest colour in the project. Use a dark neutral thread for piecing dark solids.

When machine sewing patches, align cut edges with the edge of the presser foot if it is ¼in wide. If not, place masking tape on the throat plate of the machine ¼in away from the needle to guide you in making ¼in seams. Sew along to the cut edge unless you are inserting a patch into an angle. Short seams need not be pinned unless matching is involved if the seam is long. Keep pins away from the

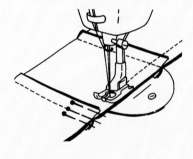

seam line. Sewing over pins is not good for sewing machine needles.

Use chain-piecing whenever possible to save time and thread. Sew one seam, but do not lift the presser foot. Do not take the piece out of the sewing machine and do not cut the thread. Instead, set up the next piece to be sewn and continue stitching. There will be small twists of thread between the two pieces. Sew all the seams you can at one time, then remove the 'chain'. Clip the threads, then press the seams.

When joining rows, make sure matching seam allowances are pressed in opposite directions to reduce bulk and make matching easier. Pin pieces together directly through stitching and to the right or left of the seam, removing the pins as you sew.

JOINING BLOCKS

Blocks joined edge to edge

Join the blocks to form strips the width of the quilt. Pin each seam very carefully, inserting a pin wherever seams meet, at right angles to the seam using a ¼in seam allowance. Join all blocks in the second row, continuing until all rows are completed. Press all seam allowances in the odd-numbered rows in one direction and all seam allowances in even-numbered rows in the opposite direction. When all rows are completed, pin two rows together so that seam lines match perfectly. Join rows in groups of two, then four, and so on until the top is completed. Press all allowances in one direction, either up or down.

Blocks joined with vertical and horizontal sashing

Join the blocks into strips with a vertical sash between each pair of blocks. Sew a horizontal piece of sashing to each strip, then join the strips to form the quilt top.

PRESSING

Press the seam allowances to one side, usually towards the darker fabric. Press quilt blocks flat and square with no puckers. To correct any problems in blocks, sashes or borders, remove a few stitches to ease puckers and re-sew.

APPLIQUE

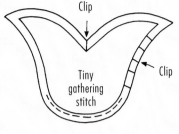

Clip

Tiny gathering stitch

Clip

Diagram 1

Diagram 2

Appliqué is not a difficult technique but basic rules do apply. Curved shapes should be smooth with no points, points should be a definite point, and there should be no puckers. Begin by marking around the template onto the right side of the fabric. Cut out the shape with a ¼in seam allowance. Turn the seam allowance under and baste. When there is a sharp curve sew a tiny running stitch just to the outside of the marked line. Gather slightly so that the curve sits well (see Diagram 1). Where there is a sharp point, mitre the corner as you are basting, and cut away any excess fabric. Be careful not to cut away too much. Pin the pieces to the background fabric making sure they are centred.

Cut a 15¾in length of thread and make a small knot. Make sure the knot sits underneath the piece being appliquéd, then bring the thread from the back through the background fabric and catch a couple of threads on the appliqué piece. When you begin to appliqué, make sure the needle enters the background fabric directly opposite

where it came out on the top piece and slightly under the piece being appliquéd (see Diagram 2). When you have completed stitching, finish off on the back with a couple of small back stitches.

ADDING MITRED BORDERS

Centre a border strip each side of the quilt top to extend equally at each end. Pin, baste, and sew strips in ¼in seams, beginning and ending at the seam line, not the outer edge of the fabric. At one corner, on the wrong side, smooth one border over the adjacent one and draw a diagonal line from the inner seam line to the point where the outer edges of the two borders cross. Reverse the two borders (the bottom one is now on top), and draw a diagonal line from the inner seam line to the point where the outer edges cross. Match the two pencil lines (fabrics right sides together), and sew through them. Cut away the excess, and press the allowances open. Repeat at the other corners of the quilt.

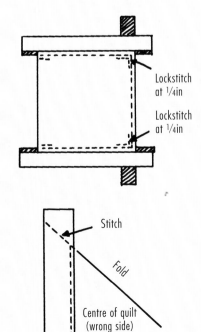

Lockstitch at ¼in

Lockstitch at ¼in

Stitch

Fold

Centre of quilt (wrong side)

BATTING

Batting is the padding that plumps up the quilt. It goes between the quilt top and the backing. There is a variety of battings on the market, ranging from natural fibres such as cotton and wool to synthetics. Most battings are available in different weights, but a thin, lightweight one is ideal for hand quilting, as it is much easier to produce small, even stitches. A thin batting also gives a more authentic appearance to traditional quilt designs. Thicker battings are useful if you want extra warmth and they can be tied rather than quilted.

BACKING

Make the quilt backing about 2in larger each side than the quilt top. The two or three lengths that need to be sewn must be seamed together. Remove the selvedges to avoid puckers and press the seam allowances open or to one side. Place the backing, wrong side up, on a flat surface. Spread quilt batting over the backing, making sure that both stay smooth and even. Place the quilt top,

right side up, on top of the batting. Pin layers as necessary to secure them while basting. Beginning in the centre, baste in an 'X'. Working outwards, baste rows 4in and 6in apart. Baste all around the edges.

MARKING FOR QUILTING

Place a quilting pattern under the quilt top. Lightly mark the design on the top, using a hard lead pencil. Mark dark-coloured fabrics with a chalk pencil. Always test water-soluble pens for removability before marking the quilt. Some quilting may be done without marking the top. Outline quilting ¼in from seam around patches or quilting in the ditch (right next to the seam on the side without the seam allowances) can be done by 'marking' the quilting line by eye. Other straight lines may also be marked as you quilt by using a piece of masking tape that is pulled away after a line is quilted along the edge.

QUILTING

Quilting is done in a short running stitch with a single strand of thread that goes through all three layers. Use a short needle (8 or 9 betweens) with about 18in thread. Make a small knot in the thread and take a first long stitch, about 1in, through the top and batting only, coming up where the quilting will begin. Tug on the thread to pull the knotted end between the layers. Take straight, even stitches that are the same size on the top and bottom of the quilt. For tiny stitches, push the needle with a thimble on your middle finger. Guide the fabric in front of the needle with the thumb of your hand

above the quilt and with the thumb and index finger of your other hand below the quilt. To end a line of quilting, take a tiny back stitch, make another small knot and pull between the layers. Make another 1in long stitch through the top and batting only and clip the thread at the surface of the quilt. Carefully pull out the basting threads when the quilting is finished.

BINDING

Trim the edges of the quilt. One of the most popular methods of binding is to cut the binding fabric into seven 3in strips, selvedge to selvedge. Join these to make one long strip and press in half along the length, wrong sides together. Sew to the quilt top, starting at the centre bottom, ½in from the raw edges. To mitre the binding, stop ½in from the corner, back stitch and take out of the machine.

Fold the binding up making a 45 degree angle with the binding strip.

Fold down, level with the edge and sew to the next corner. Repeat and overlap the ends of the binding, slip stitch in place to the back of the quilt (see diagrams on page 21). A nice finishing touch is to embroider your name, city, and date on the back of the quilt.

CARE OF QUILTS

After spending many hours making a quilt you will want to look after it in the best possible way. Remember, it may well become a future heirloom.

While you obviously want to use and enjoy your quilt, you also want to minimise the amount of wear and tear it receives. Get into the habit of folding back the quilt at night so it lies across the foot of the bed only. Or remove it entirely. In this age of electric blankets and heated waterbeds, a quilt is often decorative rather than functional. If you do need the quilt for warmth at night, place a sheet underneath it.

Turn it back over the top edge of the quilt with at least a metre turn back. This will greatly reduce soiling.

Quilts made from suitable fabrics can be washed successfully, but if you care for your quilt properly, you will reduce the need for frequent washing.

Sunlight weakens the fabric fibres and also fades the colours. If the bed receives direct sunlight it is wise to fold back the quilt or draw the curtains.

STORAGE
❖

Store your quilt by rolling or folding it and wrapping it in an old cotton pillow-case or sheet.

If it is folded, it should be refolded occasionally along different fold lines to avoid permanent creasing.

Never store in a plastic bag as air circulation is essential.

Do not place an unwrapped quilt directly on a wooden shelf as chemicals in the timber can stain the fabric.

WASHING
❖

If possible, hand wash the quilt in a large container such as the bath. Use warm, not hot water and dissolve the detergent before adding the quilt. Soak for 5 to 10 minutes then squeeze gently by hand; do not twist or wring. Rinse thoroughly in lukewarm water. If you want to use fabric conditioner make sure it is stirred into the rinse water and not poured directly onto the quilt.

If you have a washing machine large enough to take the quilt without having to cram it in, spin the quilt to remove excess water, as the excess weight of water can strain the stitching. Use a low speed spin if you have the option.

Dry the quilt outdoors away from direct sunlight. Spread it flat on a clean sheet, or drape it over a patio table. If using the clothesline, spread the quilt over several parallel lines rather than hanging the entire weight from one line.

The quilt can be machine washed if you don't have a large enough container. However, do not try to wash a large quilt in a small machine as it cannot be cleaned effectively and the lack of space can damage the quilt.

Once the quilt is dry, place it in a tumble dryer on a cool cycle to fluff up the batting.

If the quilt needs to be ironed, place it right side down on a thick towel and steam press gently on the wrong side.

Glossary

Acid-free paper
Type of tissue paper used for storing antique quilts.

Adhesive/fusible web
Fibre material that is used to fuse two layers of fabric together when pressed with an iron (ie Vliesofix).

Appliqué
A piece of fabric that is hand sewn onto a background fabric with a running stitch, slip stitch or with embroidery stitches. It can also be attached with a zigzag machine stitch.

Backing
The bottom layer of a quilt sandwich. A piece of fabric the same size as the quilt top with approximately 2in extra allowance for take up.

Basting
Large hand or machine stitches which are used to hold a quilt sandwich together while it is being quilted.

Batting
Another name for wadding or padding.

Bearding
A coating which appears on the surface of a quilt when loose fibres of padding come through the fabrics.

Beeswax
Used to strengthen thread and prevent it from tangling.

Betweens
The name given to quilting needles. The shorter the needle, the higher the number.

Bias
The grain of a fabric which is cut on the diagonal to obtain the most give or stretch. Used for curves, binding and curved edges.

Binding
A narrow strip of fabric used to finish off the edges of a quilt. Cut on the straight grain of fabric or on the bias. A binding can be made as a separate attachment, or by folding the backing over the top, or vice versa and stitching it, or by folding the edges of the top and backing inside, then sewing the folded edges together.

Bleeding
When the dye has not been firmly bonded to a fabric, the fabric loses its colour when it is washed. This is known as bleeding. Running dyes can also discolour surrounding fabrics. All fabrics should be pre-washed and tested before using.

Block
One of the square, rectangular or hexagonal pieces which make up a patchwork or appliqué quilt. Blocks are sewn together or joined with a sashing to create a quilt top.

Blocking
This is a process used to straighten a quilt block by steam, heat and pressure.

Bonded wadding/batting
Bonded wadding/batting is coated with chemicals to add a little body to a finished project and prevent it from fraying or falling apart when washed.

Border
The fabric around the outside of a quilt which can be wide or narrow, plain or pieced. Borders can give a finishing touch to a quilt and pull a design together. Many quilts, however, are made without borders.

Broderie Perse
A printed design fabric which is cut apart and sewn onto a background fabric as an appliqué.

Calico/muslin
A natural coloured plain-weave cotton fabric. Also known as muslin in America. Because of its hard wearing quality, it is almost always used as a quilt backing. Calico, in America, refers to a small floral patterned cotton fabric.

Comforter
A thick quilt made from two layers of fabric with batting in between.

Compass
Used for drawing accurate circles and making curves.

Cotton
A fabric woven from natural fibre. Cotton is a very popular fabric for quilting because it is strong and easy to work with. It is also hard wearing and washes well.

Cushion quilting
Small cushions or pillows which are individually stuffed and machine sewn together to make a quilt.

Ditch quilting/quilting in the ditch
The quilting stitches are worked in the seamlines or close to the seam and so add texture to pieced quilting. Mostly used on thick fabrics which are difficult to quilt through or on pieces where the quilting should not be seen.

Double wedding ring
Curved patchwork pieces which are sewn together to create the look of interlocked rings.

Dressmakers' carbon paper
This paper has a special waxy finish on one side, and comes in a number of colours. Good for marking, or cutting lines on fabric. Test on a piece of fabric first to make sure the marks wash out. It is best to use a matching colour so that marking is less noticeable.

Echo quilting

A line of quilting stitches running parallel to the edges of the patchwork or appliqué. More than one line of stitching is known as contour or wave quilting, and is used for Hawaiian Appliqué.

Embroidery

The embellishment of fabric with surface stitching.

Fabric glue stick

A solid adhesive which is used to join fabrics. Test a glue stick on a piece of the fabric before using.

Feed dogs

These are located on a sewing machine, within the needle plate and move up and down while sewing to help pull the fabric along.

Felt

Felt is created by pressing the fibres of a non-woven fabric, such as wool, together with heat and moisture. Felt does not fray as it has no grain. It cannot be laundered.

Filling

Wadding or batting made of cotton, wool, silk or synthetic that is used between the two layers of a quilt sandwich.

Finger-press

Flattening the fabric between the thumb and forefinger, or creasing it into position with a fingernail.

Foundation

A base of lightweight fabric, interfacing or soft paper, on which patchwork or appliqué is sewn.

Four block quilt

A quilt made up of four large patchwork or appliqué blocks, usually surrounded by a border.

Friendship quilt

Introduced to America during the 19th century, a friendship quilt was generally made for a friend who was moving away. Each person made a block, often with a message, or with the name of the town and the date. The blocks were then assembled into a quilt and presented to the person who was leaving.

Graph paper

Paper used for drafting patterns.

Grain

This is the way the threads run in a woven fabric. Lengthwise grain is in a vertical direction, crosswise grain is horizontal. The diagonal grain is called the bias. The grain of fabric should always run in the same direction on a quilt block, or on borders and sashings.

Hem

The fabric at the bottom of a project is folded over to the wrong side and slip-stitched into place to form a hem. The stitches should be invisible.

Isometric paper

A grid of triangles in sheets or pads used to draft patchwork patterns, such as diamonds, hexagons and octagons which cannot be drafted on ordinary squared graph paper.

Lace

Delicate openwork fabric made from cotton, or synthetic fibres. Often used to add dimension to a patchwork or appliqué design.

Linen

Made from the natural fibre of the flax plant, this plain-weave fabric has a slightly uneven texture. It is a strong fabric which is very absorbent. Linen is good if you want a thicker fabric for quilting but it is not generally used in patchwork quilting.

Log cabin

Strips of fabric used in patchwork, which are sewn around a central shape, usually a square.

Loose stuffing

Cotton, wool, or polyester fibres which are used to fill cushions and soft toys. Also known as Polyfil or polyester fibrefill.

Marking

Transferring a design to a piece of fabric.

Medallion quilt

A large central motif surrounded by several different borders. Medallions can be used to quilt plain fabric blocks on a patchwork or appliqué quilt or as the central point of a single fabric quilt.

Mitre

Used to finish a corner by sewing fabrics together at a 45 degree angle.

Muslin

Also known as cheesecloth. In America, muslin is a strong plain-weave natural coloured cotton fabric.

Needlemarking

Templates are placed on the quilt top after the quilt sandwich is basted together and a thick, blunt yarn needle is used to mark around the edges, creating creases which are then quilted. This type of marking is popular with advanced quilters who don't need to mark the entire quilt before they start.

Notch

A triangle cut out of the edge of a patchwork template. Notches are marked on the fabric to match the triangle when the pieces are sewn together.

Organdy

Transparent cotton fabric with permanent stiffening.

Organza

A fine transparent silk or synthetic fabric with a slight sheen.

Padding

Also called wadding or batting. The middle layer of a quilt sandwich. Can be bought in sheets or as loose stuffing. Made from cotton, wool, silk or synthetic fibres.

Patch

A piece of fabric used to make a patch-work pattern. A small piece of fabric used to cover a hole.

Perlé Coton

A cotton embroidery thread that has a silky appearance. Available in a variety of colours and diameters. An excellent thread to use for embroidering crazy patchwork or for tying quilts.

Pieced quilt

A quilt which is made up of patches.

Pin baste

Basting layers of fabric together with straight pins instead of stitches. Pin basting is used for simple projects. The term is also used to secure the three layers of a quilt together with safety pins while quilting.

Polyester

A synthetic fabric that is woven or knitted into a number of different cloth weights. Also used to make strong thread.

Polyfil

Trade name for loose stuffing used for filling cushions and soft toys. Also known as polyester fibrefill.

Press

To flatten a fabric with a steam iron, lift it and place it down again. Do not slide the iron over the fabric.

Presser foot

Holds the fabric firmly onto the needle plate on a sewing machine so that the needle passes through the fabric.

Quilt

A bed cover composed of a top, batting and backing which is then quilted together or tied.

Quilting frame

A four-sided frame which holds the three layers of a quilt tightly together to assist with even stitching.

Quilting hoop

A round or oval frame used to hold small pieces of a quilt taut for even stitching.

Quilting stitch

A running stitch that is sewn through the quilt top, batting and backing to hold the three layers together. Quilting stitches can be worked in some form of design or at random.

Reducing glass

Used for viewing patchwork before it is sewn together to see how the finished design will look.

Remnant

A small piece of leftover fabric. Remnants are usually reduced in price for a quick sale. Always check that remnants do not have seconds, or irregularities in them, before you buy.

Reverse appliqué

The opposite of appliqué. A layer of fabric is removed to reveal the design.

Rotary cutter

A tool used to cut up to six layers of fabric at one time. The fabric is placed on a cutting mat and cut with a sharp circular blade which is drawn along the edge of a thick plastic ruler.

Rotary ruler

A thick clear plastic ruler printed with lines exactly ¼in apart. It is used with a rotary cutter. There are also diagonal lines indicating 45° and 60° marked on most rotary rulers.

Sampler quilt

A quilt made up blocks which are all different. Sampler quilts are used to teach different techniques.

Sashing

Strips of fabric used to join blocks in a quilt top. Sashing is also used to frame blocks, to enhance a quilt design and to increase the size of your quilt.

Satin

A silk, cotton or synthetic fabric with a sheen. Satin fabric is slippery and can be difficult to work with.

Sawtooth edging

Squares of fabric folded into triangles that are inserted into the edges of a quilt to finish it.

Scrap quilt

A quilt made from pieces of fabric scraps which are bright and colourful because of the range of fabrics used to create them.

Seconds

An irregularity or fault in a length of fabric. This could be a knot or a slub, dirt or grease. Seconds can be used for patchwork and appliqué but always cut out the fault before you start measuring.

Selvedges

These are the finished edges of a piece of fabric. Selvedges should not be used in patchwork because the threads are woven more than the rest of the fabric and may shrink when the fabric is washed.

Setting-in

A technique in which one patchwork shape is sewn into an angle formed by two other shapes which are joined.

Silk

A natural fibre which is strong and lustrous. It can be woven into a variety of fabrics of different weights and texture.

Sleeve

A fabric casing sewn to the backing of a quilt so it can be hung.

Stay stitching

Machine stitches sewn just inside a seam allowance to stabilise the edge of the fabric. These stitches should be invisible.

Strip

A long narrow piece of fabric.

Strip piecing

Strips of fabric which are sewn together to create an abstract design or picture.

Tacking

Also known as basting. Invisible stitches worked on top of one another which are used to secure fabric layers together.

Templates

A pattern piece used to mark fabrics for patchwork, appliqué and quilting. Usually made of strong cardboard or plastic. Templates can be kept and reused.

Tied quilting

A quick way to hold the quilt sandwich together without using the traditional running stitches. The thread is inserted through the quilt at regular intervals and tied in a square knot or bow. An alternative is to secure the quilt sandwich with buttons.

Top

The top layer of a quilt sandwich made of patchwork, appliqué or one piece of fabric. The other two layers are made of batting and backing.

Unpicker/seam ripper

A sharp, curved tool with a pointed tip that is used to undo stitching.

Wadding

Another term for batting/padding.

Warp

Vertical threads running through the length of a woven fabric.

Weft

The horizontal threads in a woven fabric.

Window template

The outline of the patchwork or appliqué shape with a ¼in seam allowance. The template appears as a window through which the fabric is seen.

Wool

A natural fibre woven from the sheep's fleece. Woollen fabrics are warm, resilient and absorbent. Many early quilts were made from woollen fabrics.

Index

Quilting projects are in italics